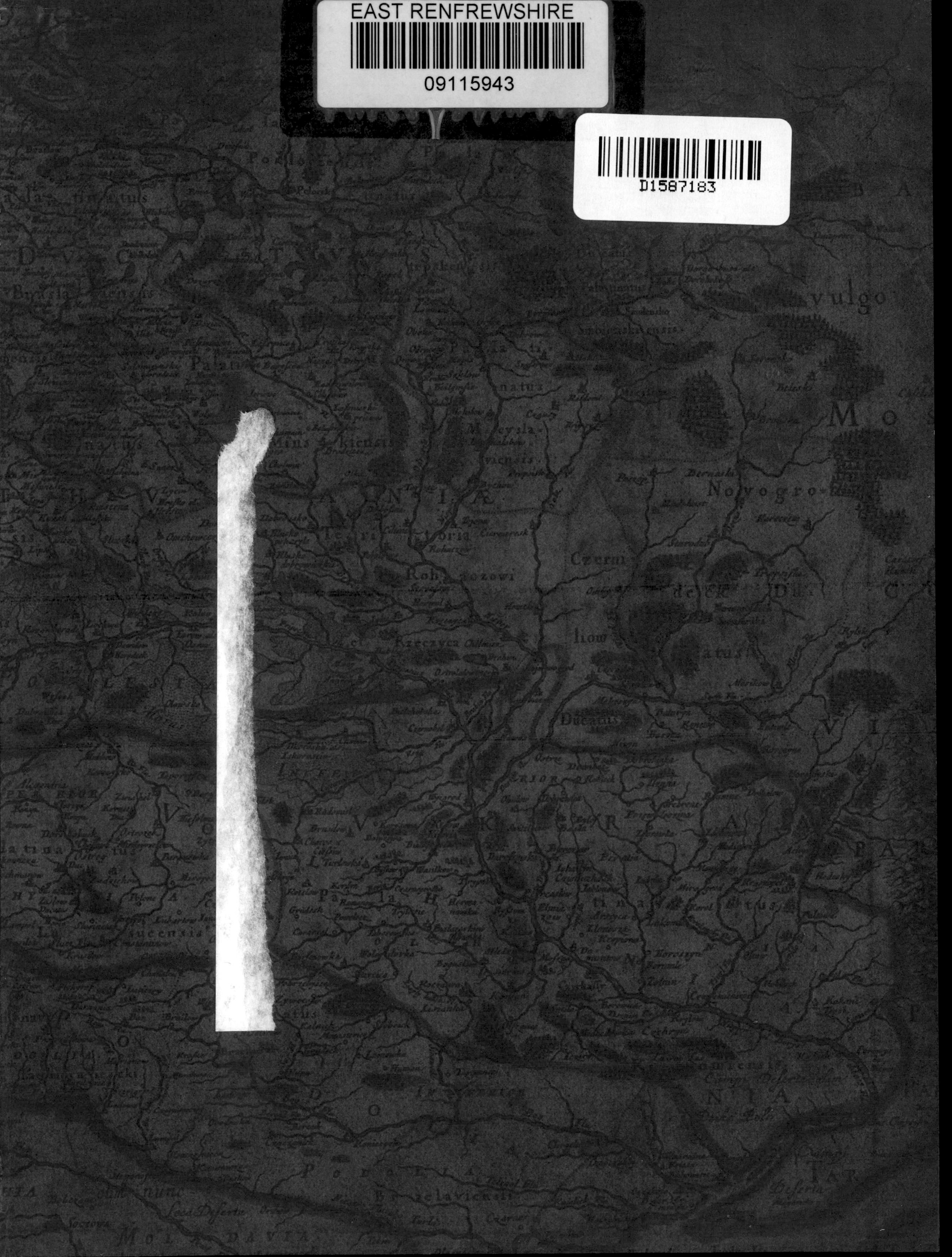
vulgo
Ducatus

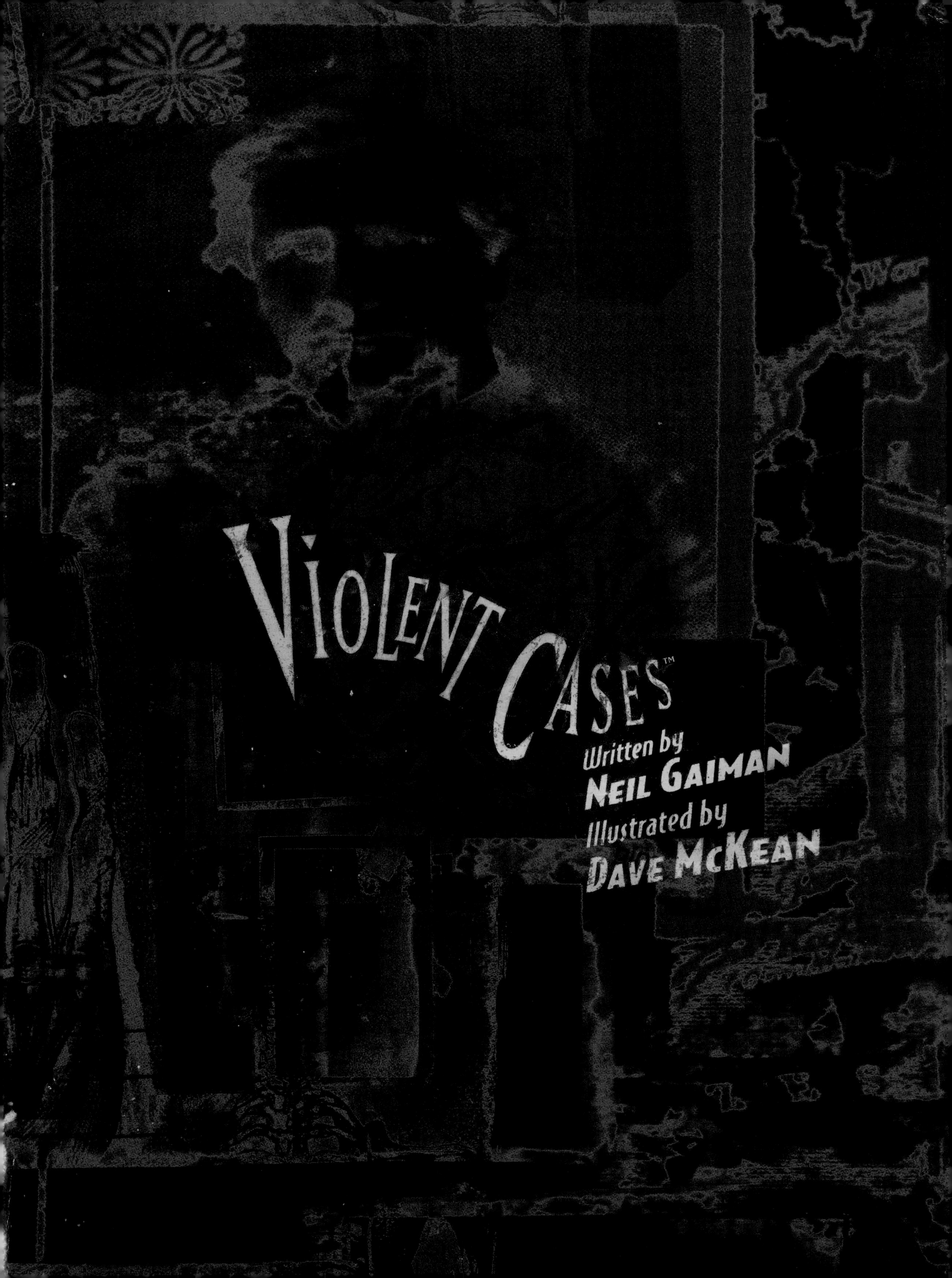
VIOLENT CASES™
Written by
NEIL GAIMAN
Illustrated by
DAVE McKEAN

PRESIDENT & PUBLISHER
Mike Richardson

DARK HORSE EDITION EDITOR
Sierra Hahn

DARK HORSE EDITION ASSISTANT EDITOR
Freddye Lins

Neil Hankerson **EXECUTIVE VICE PRESIDENT** Tom Weddle **CHIEF FINANCIAL OFFICER**
Randy Stradley **VICE PRESIDENT OF PUBLISHING** Michael Martens **VICE PRESIDENT OF BOOK TRADE SALES**
Anita Nelson **VICE PRESIDENT OF BUSINESS AFFAIRS** Scott Allie **EDITOR IN CHIEF** Matt Parkinson
VICE PRESIDENT OF MARKETING David Scroggy **VICE PRESIDENT OF PRODUCT DEVELOPMENT**
Dale LaFountain **VICE PRESIDENT OF INFORMATION TECHNOLOGY**
Darlene Vogel **SENIOR DIRECTOR OF PRINT, DESIGN, AND PRODUCTION** Ken Lizzi **GENERAL COUNSEL**
Davey Estrada **EDITORIAL DIRECTOR** Chris Warner **SENIOR BOOKS EDITOR** Diana Schutz **EXECUTIVE EDITOR**
Cary Grazzini **DIRECTOR OF PRINT AND DEVELOPMENT** Lia Ribacchi **ART DIRECTOR** Cara Niece **DIRECTOR OF SCHEDULING**
Tim Wiesch **DIRECTOR OF INTERNATIONAL LICENSING** Mark Bernardi **DIRECTOR OF DIGITAL PUBLISHING**

Special thanks to Cary Grazzini and Diana Schutz at Dark Horse Comics, Jay Austin, and Shield Bonnichsen.

VIOLENT CASES™

PUBLISHED BY DARK HORSE BOOKS
A DIVISION OF DARK HORSE COMICS, INC.
10956 SE MAIN STREET
MILWAUKIE, OR 97222

DarkHorse.com

International Licensing: (503) 905-2377
To find a comics shop in your area, call the Comic Shop Locator Service toll-free at 1-888-266-4226.

First Dark Horse edition: October 2003
First Dark Horse hardcover edition: November 2013
ISBN 978-1-61655-210-7

1 3 5 7 9 10 8 6 4 2
Printed in China

INTRODUCTION
From the 1997 reissue of Violent Cases
PAUL GRAVETT

Ten years ago Peter Stanbury and I, as coeditors of *Escape* magazine since 1983, had always kept a close eye on all that was happening in the British small press comics scene. And a lot was happening. *Escape* had sprouted and blossomed directly out of the Fast Fiction mail-order and comic mart network I had started for the small press in 1981. Eddie Campbell, Phil Elliott, Glenn Dakin, Myra Hancock, and Ed Pinsent were just some of the individualistic young creators I had first spotted developing in their own self-published comics. Their comics just could not fit into *2000 AD*, or Marvel/DC, or *pssst!*, or *Warrior*, or even the conventions of underground comix. If you really believe in what you are doing, you'll create it, self-publish it if necessary, rather than ape the tired clichés and genres that blinkered editors tell you the readers want. In the small press, there was a different, distinct, uncompromising, and rather British attitude, and *Escape* brought them together.

Dave McKean had stood out to me straight away in his self-published comics *Meanwhile . . .* starting in 1984, although to me these stories didn't quite live up to his graphic skills. Still, definitely someone to watch. I first met Neil Gaiman in the chic offices of some dilettante business suits, who ended up failing to finance a new comics magazine called *Borderline*. Out of this, Dave and Neil met each other and came to me with a proposal for *Escape*, a five-page story that just kept growing.

We'd meet at the Central Hall Westminster Comic Marts or in a pub next door, and I'd read or hear about the next page and share in their interchange of ideas. Neil and Dave would not deny that they started by being influenced respectively by Alan Moore and Bill Sienkiewicz (notably, in Dave's case, Sienkiewicz's 1982 breakthrough story "Hit It" in *Moon Knight* #26). But in tandem, they quickly evolved their own voice. Something special was being nurtured here, a writer-artist alchemy that has continued to deepen and diversify. They were finding ways of conveying what I felt comics should start to do, showing those intimate, subtle emotions of everyday life, those minute incidents and personal yet universal memories that Eddie Campbell was recording so tellingly in his *Alec* biographic novels, also from *Escape*. It's no coincidence that this observation and humanity would later form *Cages*, Dave's solo debut as a writer-artist.

There was something in *Violent Cases*. It had to see print. Back in 1987, in the midst of *Maus*, *Dark Knight*, *Watchmen*, and all the slightly mad optimism about "comics growing up," *Escape* made the difficult adjustments from the freedom and financial precipices of creative independence to being published and backed by Titan Books, a comic publisher whose whole line until then was built on safe, sure-fire reprints and repackaging. For all of us, and for them too, *Violent Cases*, a creator-driven and originated, experimental, nongenre "graphic novel/fiction" by two unknowns, was a radical departure, a leap of faith. It finally appeared in October 1987, and rave reviews, DC contracts, success, and acclaim swiftly followed.

Ten years on, this book still has a lot to show people. Neil later said that *Violent Cases* "was done for us. It was done because we wanted it to be done." I hope it will encourage more writers, artists, editors, and publishers, whether newcomers or old hands, to create comics out of passion and commitment, to tell stories that need to be told, and above all to take that leap of faith.

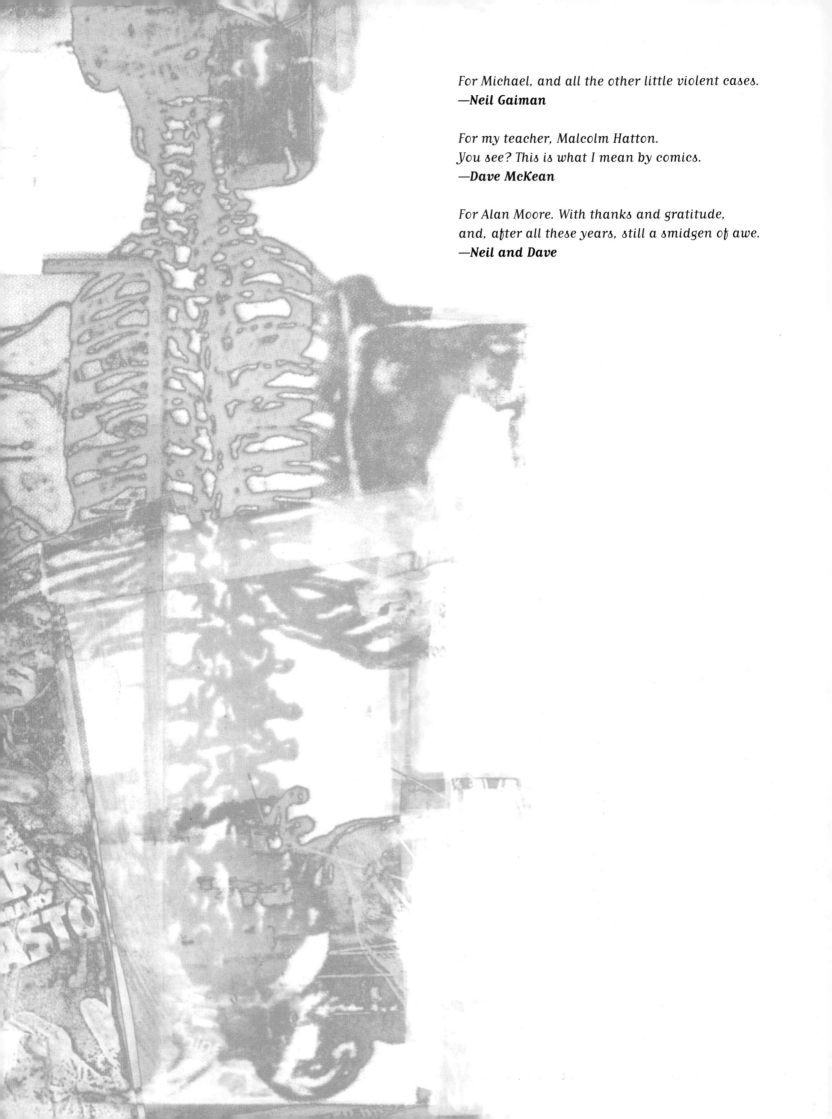

For Michael, and all the other little violent cases.
—*Neil Gaiman*

For my teacher, Malcolm Hatton.
You see? This is what I mean by comics.
—*Dave McKean*

For Alan Moore. With thanks and gratitude,
and, after all these years, still a smidgen of awe.
—*Neil and Dave*

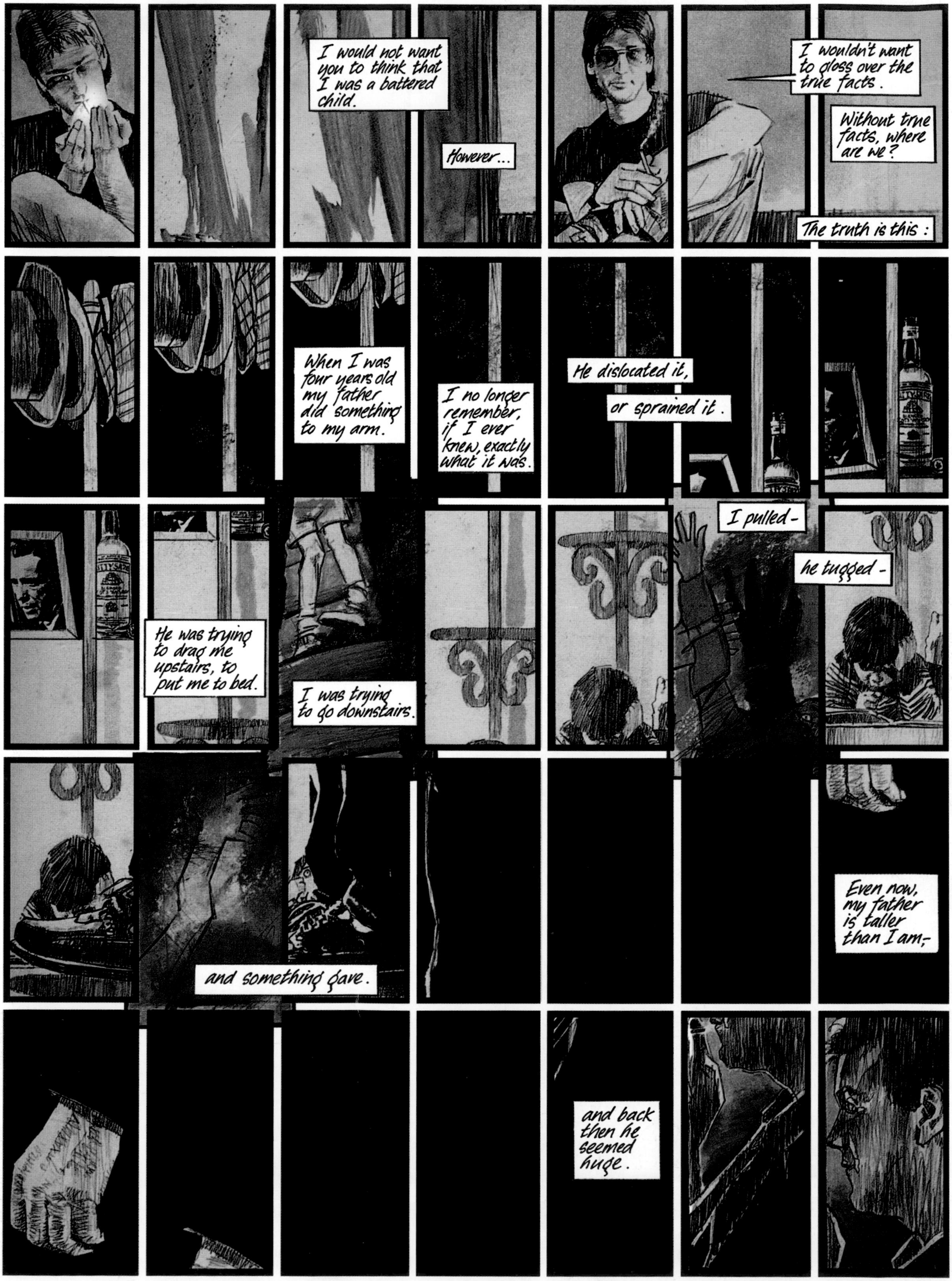
I would not want you to think that I was a battered child.
However...
I wouldn't want to gloss over the true facts.
Without true facts, where are we?
The truth is this:
When I was four years old my father did something to my arm.
I no longer remember, if I ever knew, exactly what it was.
He dislocated it,
or sprained it.
He was trying to drag me upstairs, to put me to bed.
I was trying to go downstairs.
I pulled-
he tugged-
and something gave.
Even now, my father is taller than I am;-
and back then he seemed huge.

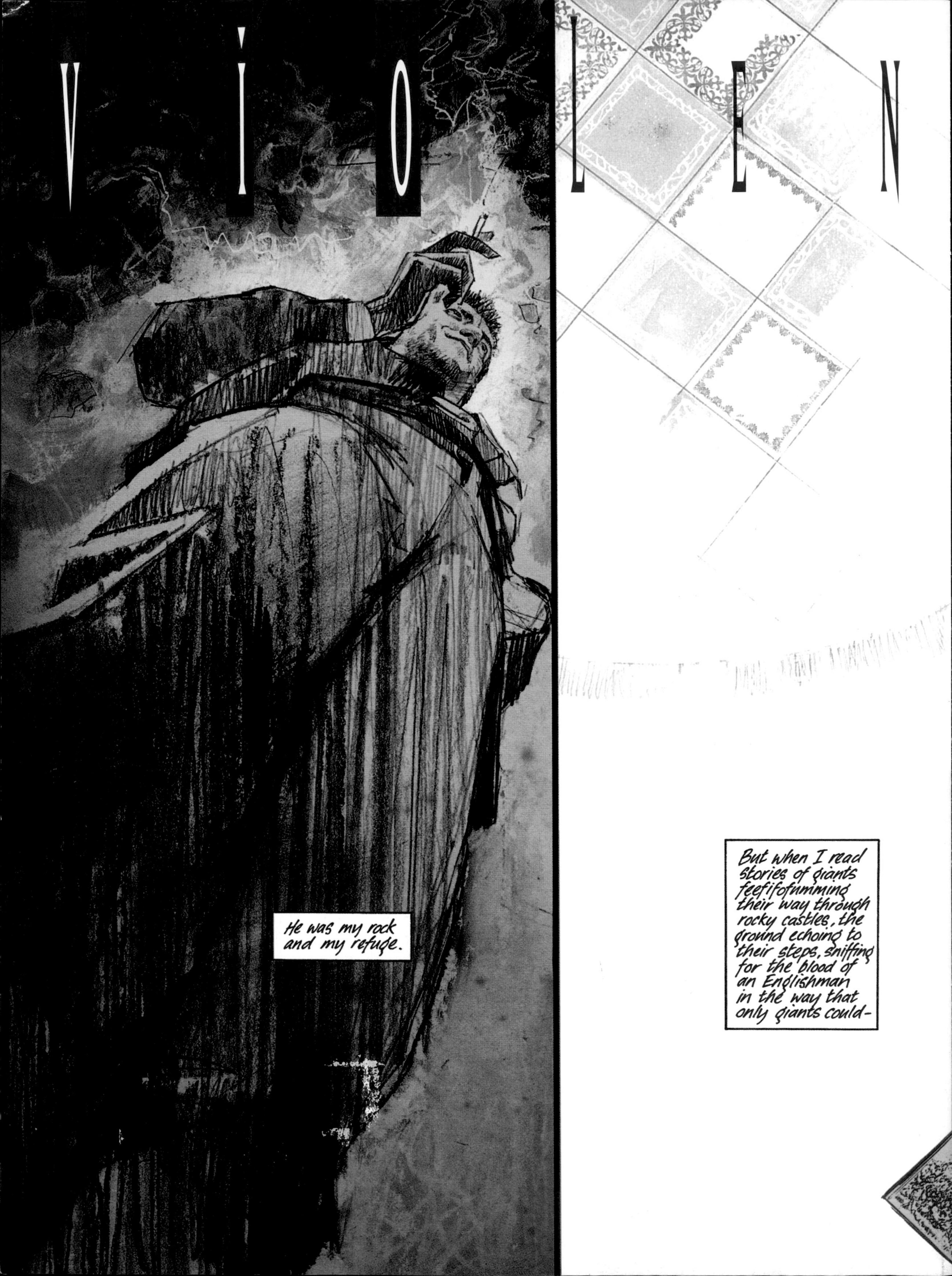
V I O L E N
He was my rock and my refuge.
But when I read stories of giants feefifofumming their way through rocky castles, the ground echoing to their steps, sniffing for the blood of an Englishman in the way that only giants could-

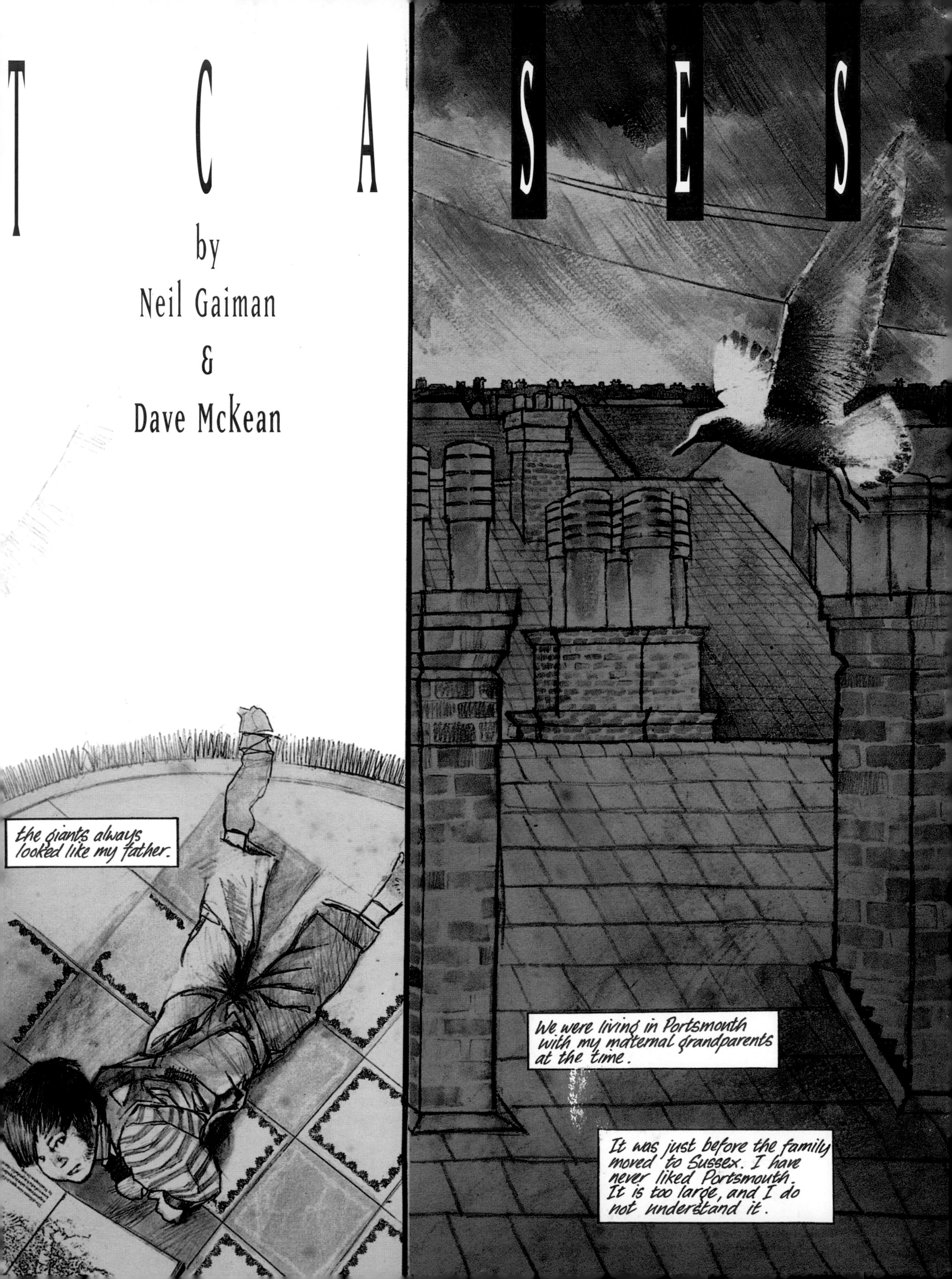
T C A
S E S
by
Neil Gaiman
&
Dave McKean
the giants always looked like my father.
We were living in Portsmouth with my maternal grandparents at the time.
It was just before the family moved to Sussex. I have never liked Portsmouth. It is too large, and I do not understand it.

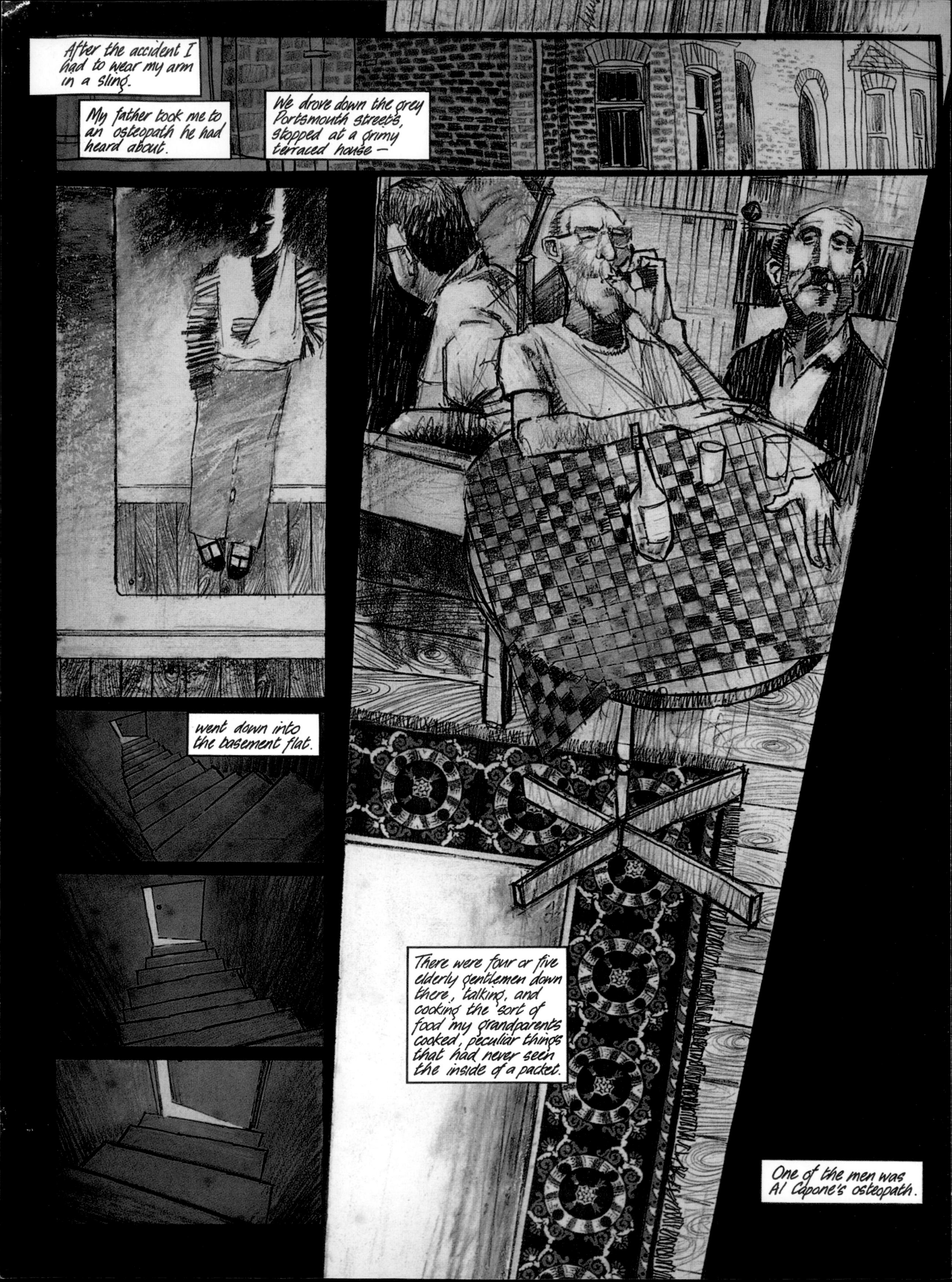
After the accident I had to wear my arm in a sling.
My father took me to an osteopath he had heard about.
We drove down the grey Portsmouth streets, stopped at a grimy terraced house –
went down into the basement flat.
There were four or five elderly gentlemen down there, talking, and cooking the sort of food my grandparents cooked, peculiar things that had never seen the inside of a packet.
One of the men was Al Capone's osteopath.

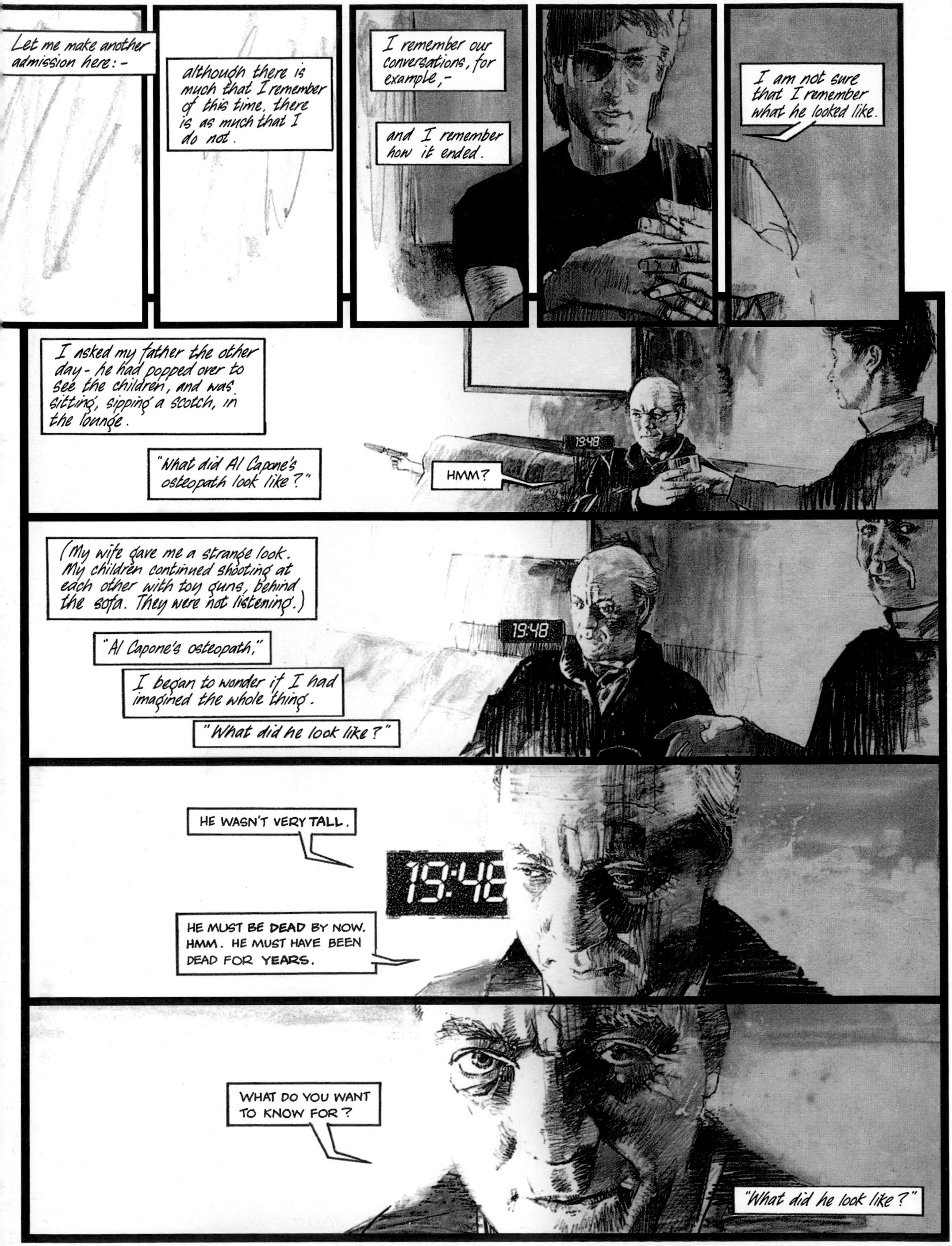
Let me make another admission here:-
although there is much that I remember of this time, there is as much that I do not.
I remember our conversations, for example,-
and I remember how it ended.
I am not sure that I remember what he looked like.
I asked my father the other day - he had popped over to see the children, and was sitting, sipping a scotch, in the lounge.
"What did Al Capone's osteopath look like?"
19:48
HMM?
(My wife gave me a strange look. My children continued shooting at each other with toy guns, behind the sofa. They were not listening.)
19:48
"Al Capone's osteopath,"
I began to wonder if I had imagined the whole thing.
"What did he look like?"
HE WASN'T VERY TALL.
HE MUST BE DEAD BY NOW. HMM. HE MUST HAVE BEEN DEAD FOR YEARS.
WHAT DO YOU WANT TO KNOW FOR?
"What did he look like?"

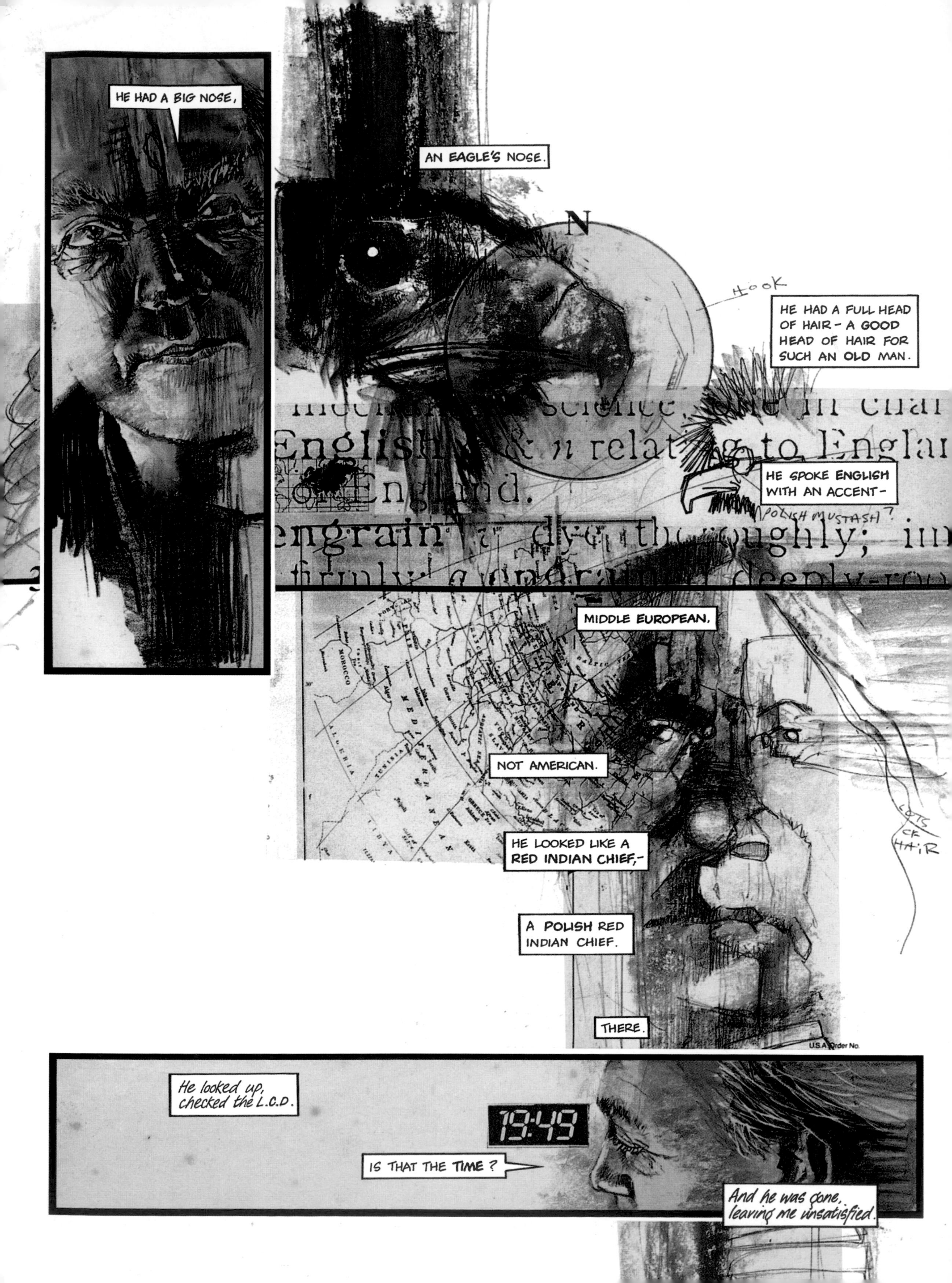
HE HAD A BIG NOSE,
AN EAGLE'S NOSE.
HOOK
HE HAD A FULL HEAD OF HAIR – A GOOD HEAD OF HAIR FOR SUCH AN OLD MAN.
HE SPOKE ENGLISH WITH AN ACCENT –
POLISH MUSTASH?
MIDDLE EUROPEAN.
NOT AMERICAN.
HE LOOKED LIKE A RED INDIAN CHIEF, –
LOTS OF HAIR
A POLISH RED INDIAN CHIEF.
THERE.
U.S.A. Order No.
He looked up, checked the L.C.D.
19:49
IS THAT THE TIME?
And he was gone, leaving me unsatisfied.

I am not sure that his description agrees with my own memories.

Yet my memories are blurred, vaseline-filtered :

I remember an owl-like man, chubby and friendly, —

peering at me over thick spectacles while he inspected my back and arm.

Who was this?

Not the gaunt grey chief of my father's description.

A doctor perhaps, —

or no-one at all:

I synthesise the two pictures into a third, undoubtedly imaginary.

I was four and a half.

We were alone in the consulting room. The osteopath took off my jumper and examined my arm and shoulder.

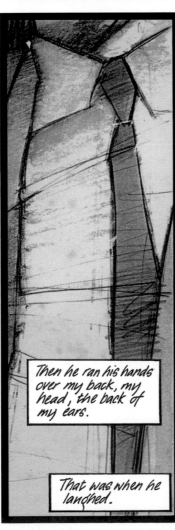

Then he ran his hands over my back, my head, the back of my ears.

That was when he laughed.

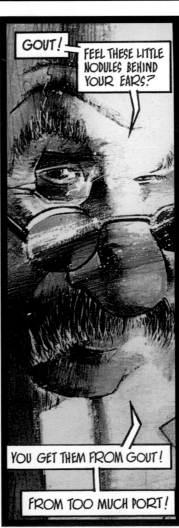

GOUT!

FEEL THESE LITTLE NODULES BEHIND YOUR EARS?

YOU GET THEM FROM GOUT!

FROM TOO MUCH PORT!

He thought this incredibly funny.

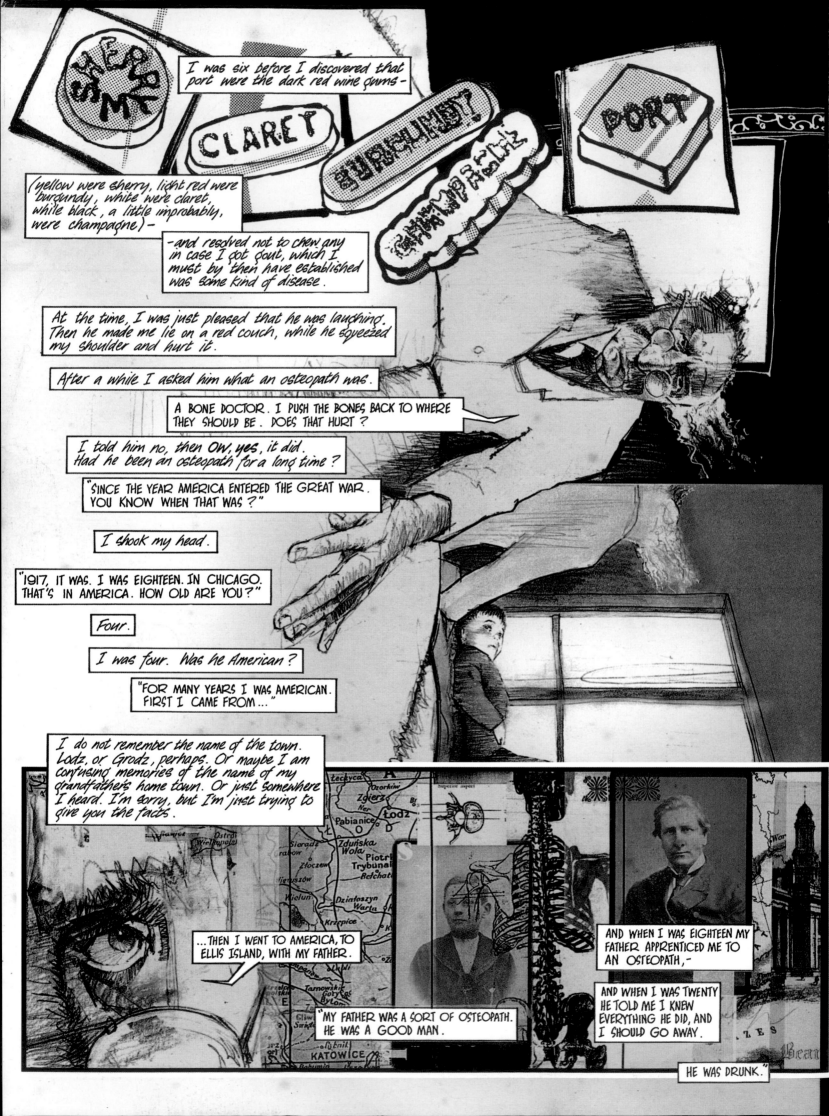

I was six before I discovered that port were the dark red wine gums—

HENRY SAM

CLARET

BURGUNDY?

CHAMPAGNE

PORT

(yellow were sherry, light red were burgundy, white were claret, while black, a little improbably, were champagne)—

—and resolved not to chew any in case I got gout, which I must by then have established was some kind of disease.

At the time, I was just pleased that he was laughing. Then he made me lie on a red couch, while he squeezed my shoulder and hurt it.

After a while I asked him what an osteopath was.

A BONE DOCTOR. I PUSH THE BONES BACK TO WHERE THEY SHOULD BE. DOES THAT HURT?

I told him no, then OW, yes, it did. Had he been an osteopath for a long time?

"SINCE THE YEAR AMERICA ENTERED THE GREAT WAR. YOU KNOW WHEN THAT WAS?"

I shook my head.

"1917, IT WAS. I WAS EIGHTEEN. IN CHICAGO. THAT'S IN AMERICA. HOW OLD ARE YOU?"

Four.

I was four. Was he American?

"FOR MANY YEARS I WAS AMERICAN. FIRST I CAME FROM..."

I do not remember the name of the town. Lodz, or Grodz, perhaps. Or maybe I am confusing memories of the name of my grandfather's home town. Or just somewhere I heard. I'm sorry, but I'm just trying to give you the facts.

...THEN I WENT TO AMERICA, TO ELLIS ISLAND, WITH MY FATHER.

"MY FATHER WAS A SORT OF OSTEOPATH. HE WAS A GOOD MAN.

AND WHEN I WAS EIGHTEEN MY FATHER APPRENTICED ME TO AN OSTEOPATH,—

AND WHEN I WAS TWENTY HE TOLD ME I KNEW EVERYTHING HE DID, AND I SHOULD GO AWAY.

HE WAS DRUNK."

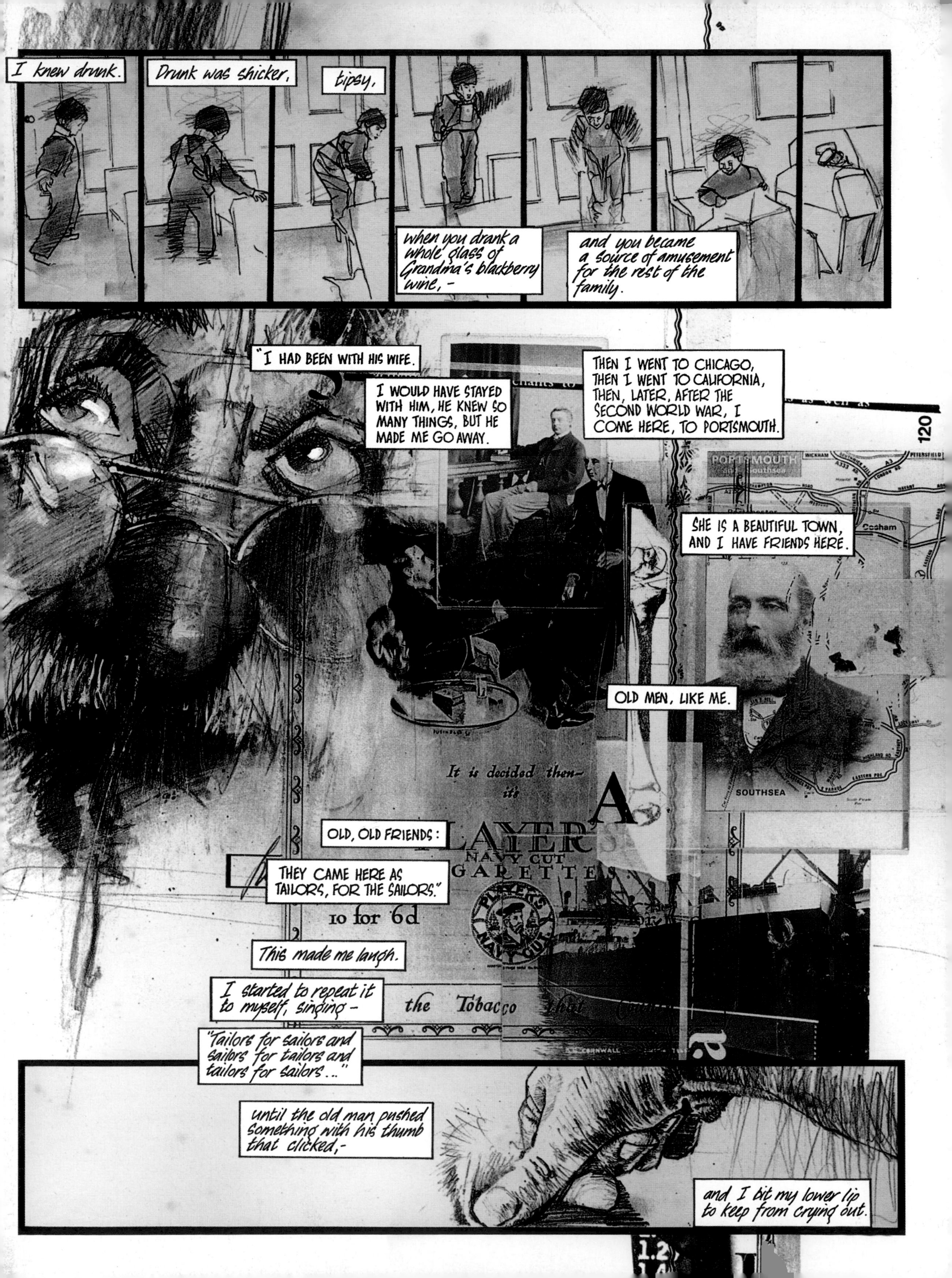
I knew drunk.
Drunk was shicker,
tipsy,
when you drank a whole glass of Grandma's blackberry wine, -
and you became a source of amusement for the rest of the family.
"I HAD BEEN WITH HIS WIFE.
I WOULD HAVE STAYED WITH HIM, HE KNEW SO MANY THINGS, BUT HE MADE ME GO AWAY.
THEN I WENT TO CHICAGO, THEN I WENT TO CALIFORNIA, THEN, LATER, AFTER THE SECOND WORLD WAR, I COME HERE, TO PORTSMOUTH.
SHE IS A BEAUTIFUL TOWN, AND I HAVE FRIENDS HERE.
OLD MEN, LIKE ME.
OLD, OLD FRIENDS:
THEY CAME HERE AS TAILORS, FOR THE SAILORS."
This made me laugh.
I started to repeat it to myself, singing -
"Tailors for sailors and sailors for tailors and tailors for sailors..."
until the old man pushed something with his thumb that clicked, -
and I bit my lower lip to keep from crying out.
It is decided then— it's
10 for 6d
the Tobacco
PORTSMOUTH
SOUTHSEA
120

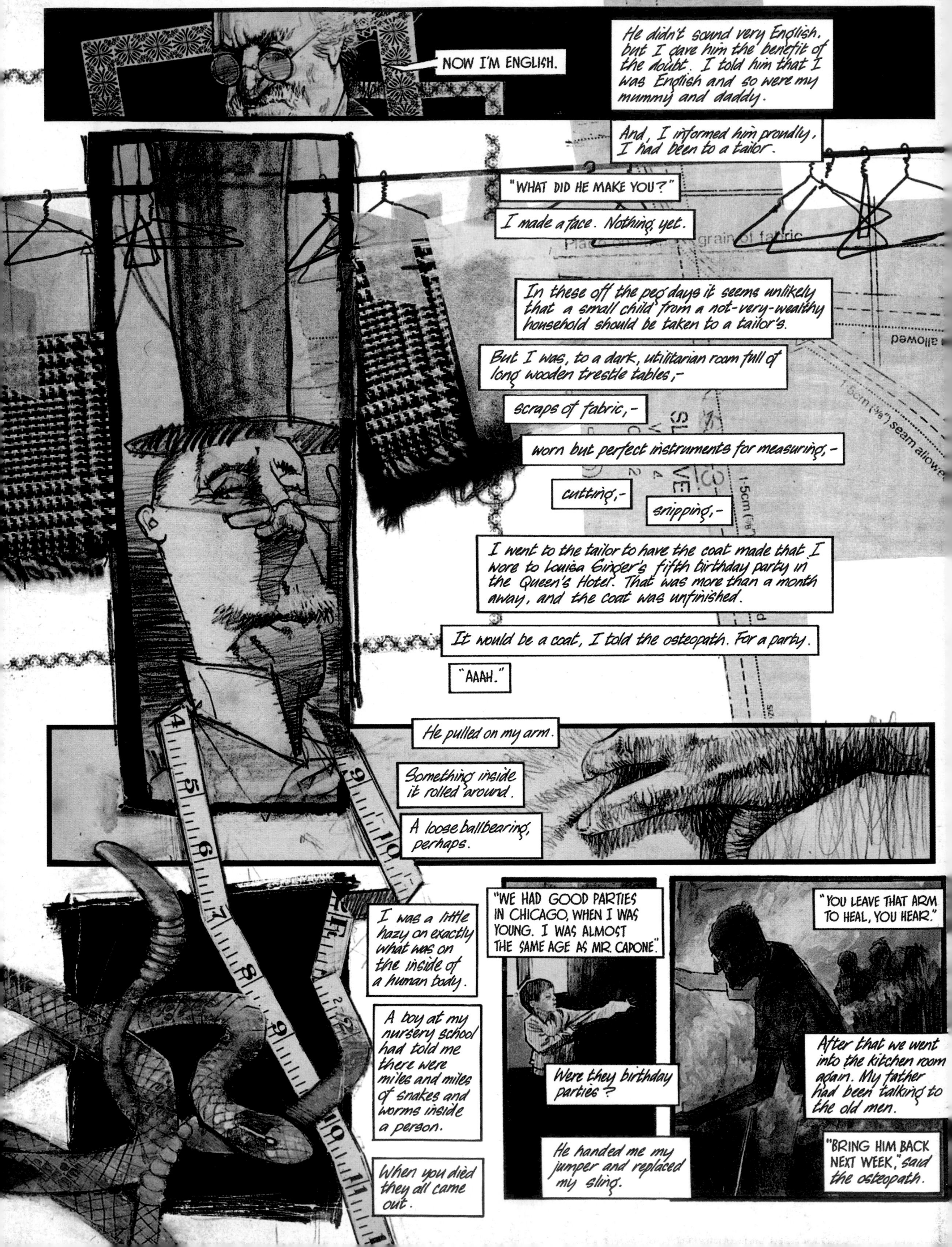
NOW I'M ENGLISH.
He didn't sound very English, but I gave him the benefit of the doubt. I told him that I was English and so were my mummy and daddy.
And, I informed him proudly, I had been to a tailor.
"WHAT DID HE MAKE YOU?"
I made a face. Nothing yet.
In these off the peg days it seems unlikely that a small child from a not-very-wealthy household should be taken to a tailor's.
But I was, to a dark, utilitarian room full of long wooden trestle tables,-
scraps of fabric,-
worn but perfect instruments for measuring,-
cutting,-
snipping,-
I went to the tailor to have the coat made that I wore to Louisa Singer's fifth birthday party in the Queen's Hotel. That was more than a month away, and the coat was unfinished.
It would be a coat, I told the osteopath. For a party.
"AAAH."
He pulled on my arm.
Something inside it rolled around.
A loose ballbearing, perhaps.
I was a little hazy on exactly what was on the inside of a human body.
A boy at my nursery school had told me there were miles and miles of snakes and worms inside a person.
When you died they all came out.
"WE HAD GOOD PARTIES IN CHICAGO, WHEN I WAS YOUNG. I WAS ALMOST THE SAME AGE AS MR. CAPONE".
Were they birthday parties?
He handed me my jumper and replaced my sling.
"YOU LEAVE THAT ARM TO HEAL, YOU HEAR."
After that we went into the kitchen room again. My father had been talking to the old men.
"BRING HIM BACK NEXT WEEK," said the osteopath.

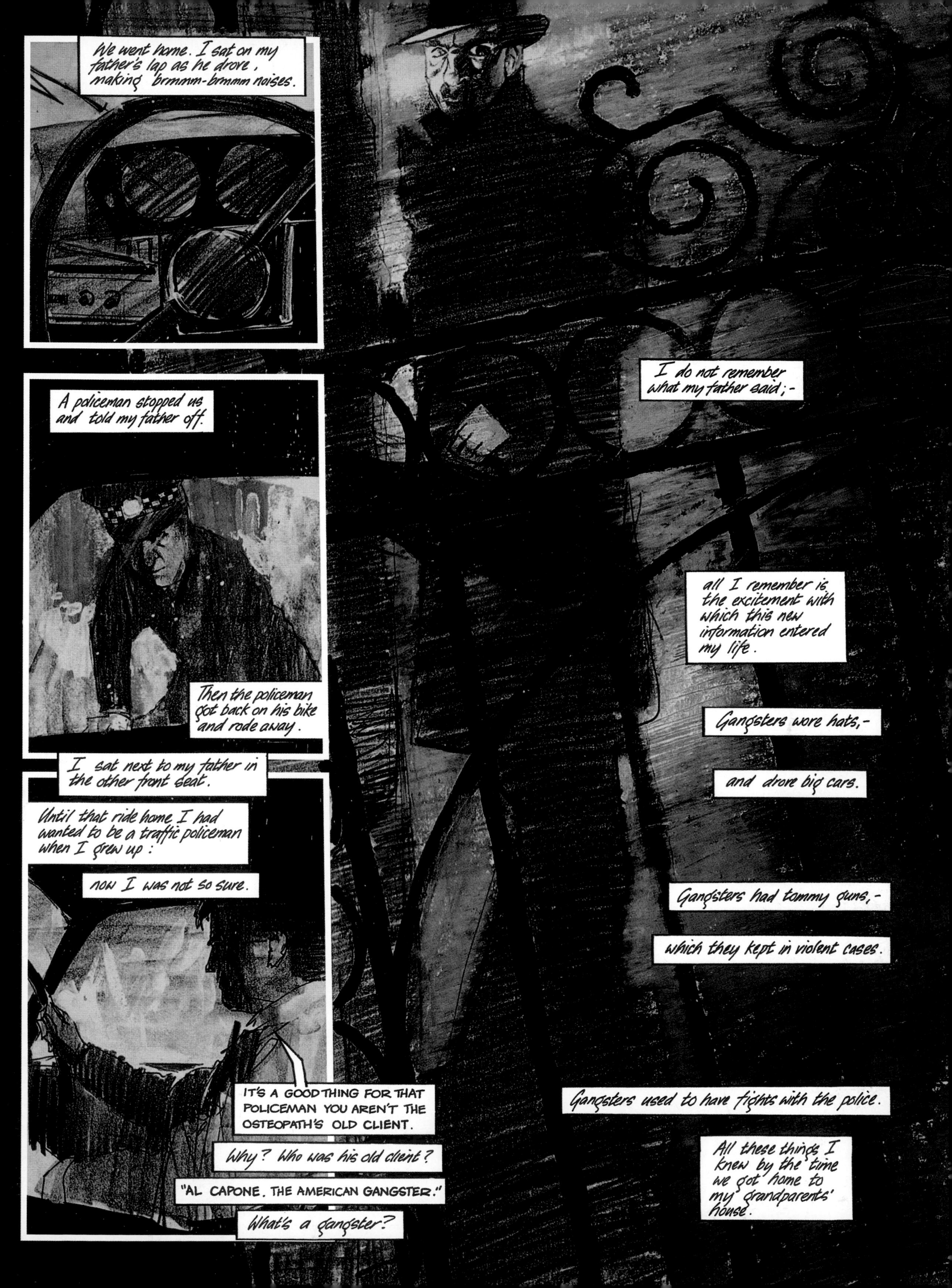
We went home. I sat on my father's lap as he drove, making brmmm-brmmm noises.
A policeman stopped us and told my father off.
Then the policeman got back on his bike and rode away.
I sat next to my father in the other front seat.
Until that ride home I had wanted to be a traffic policeman when I grew up:
now I was not so sure.
IT'S A GOOD THING FOR THAT POLICEMAN YOU AREN'T THE OSTEOPATH'S OLD CLIENT.
Why? Who was his old client?
"AL CAPONE. THE AMERICAN GANGSTER."
What's a gangster?
I do not remember what my father said;-
all I remember is the excitement with which this new information entered my life.
Gangsters wore hats,-
and drove big cars.
Gangsters had tommy guns,-
which they kept in violent cases.
Gangsters used to have fights with the police.
All these things I knew by the time we got home to my grandparents' house.

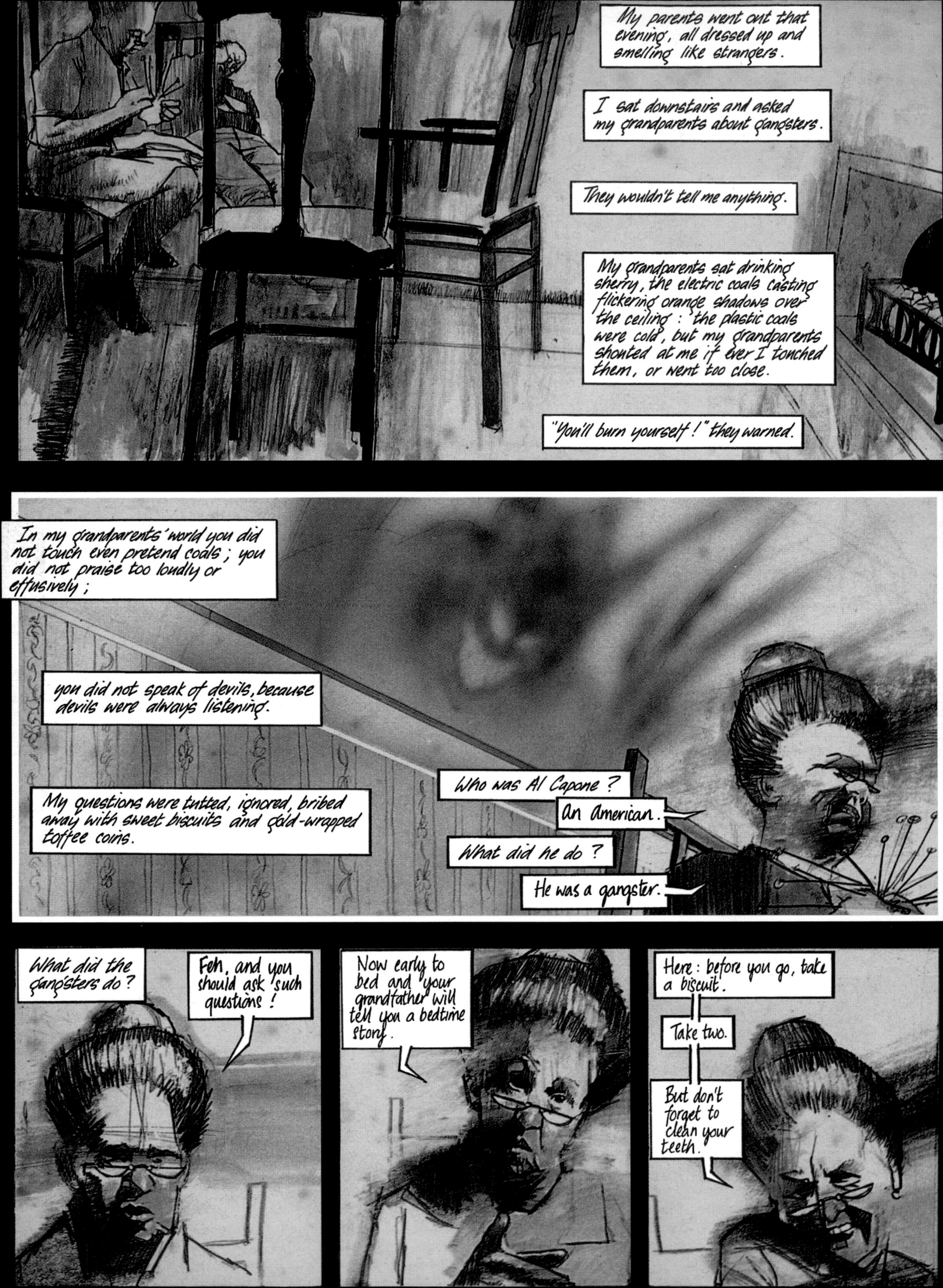
My parents went out that evening, all dressed up and smelling like strangers.
I sat downstairs and asked my grandparents about gangsters.
They wouldn't tell me anything.
My grandparents sat drinking sherry, the electric coals casting flickering orange shadows over the ceiling : the plastic coals were cold, but my grandparents shouted at me if ever I touched them, or went too close.
"You'll burn yourself !" they warned.
In my grandparents' world you did not touch even pretend coals ; you did not praise too loudly or effusively ;
you did not speak of devils, because devils were always listening.
My questions were tutted, ignored, bribed away with sweet biscuits and gold-wrapped toffee coins.
Who was Al Capone ?
An American.
What did he do ?
He was a gangster.
What did the gangsters do ?
Feh, and you should ask such questions !
Now early to bed and your grandfather will tell you a bedtime story.
Here : before you go, take a biscuit.
Take two.
But don't forget to clean your teeth.

...was sweating;

my mother's make-up was smudged.

The basement kitchen was empty, so my father sat and read an old copy of PUNCH while the osteopath took me into his rooms and examined my arm.

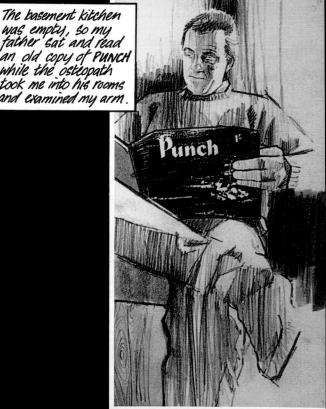

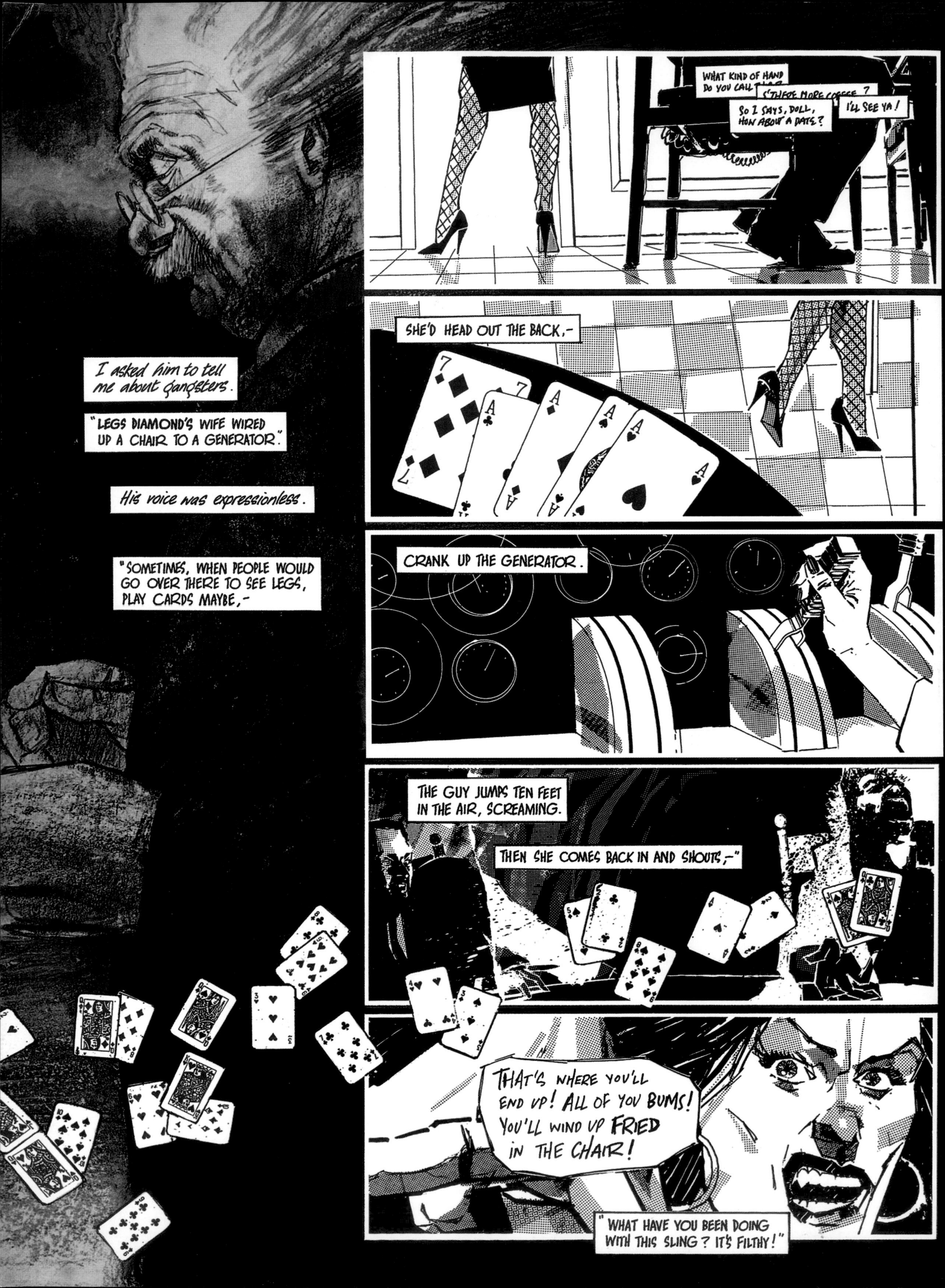
I asked him to tell me about gangsters.
"LEGS DIAMOND'S WIFE WIRED UP A CHAIR TO A GENERATOR."
His voice was expressionless.
"SOMETIMES, WHEN PEOPLE WOULD GO OVER THERE TO SEE LEGS, PLAY CARDS MAYBE,-
WHAT KIND OF HAND DO YOU CALL
S'THERE MORE COFFEE?
SO I SAYS, DOLL, HOW ABOUT A DATE?
I'LL SEE YA!
SHE'D HEAD OUT THE BACK,-
CRANK UP THE GENERATOR.
THE GUY JUMPS TEN FEET IN THE AIR, SCREAMING.
THEN SHE COMES BACK IN AND SHOUTS,-"
THAT'S WHERE YOU'LL END UP! ALL OF YOU BUMS! YOU'LL WIND UP FRIED IN THE CHAIR!
"WHAT HAVE YOU BEEN DOING WITH THIS SLING? IT'S FILTHY!"

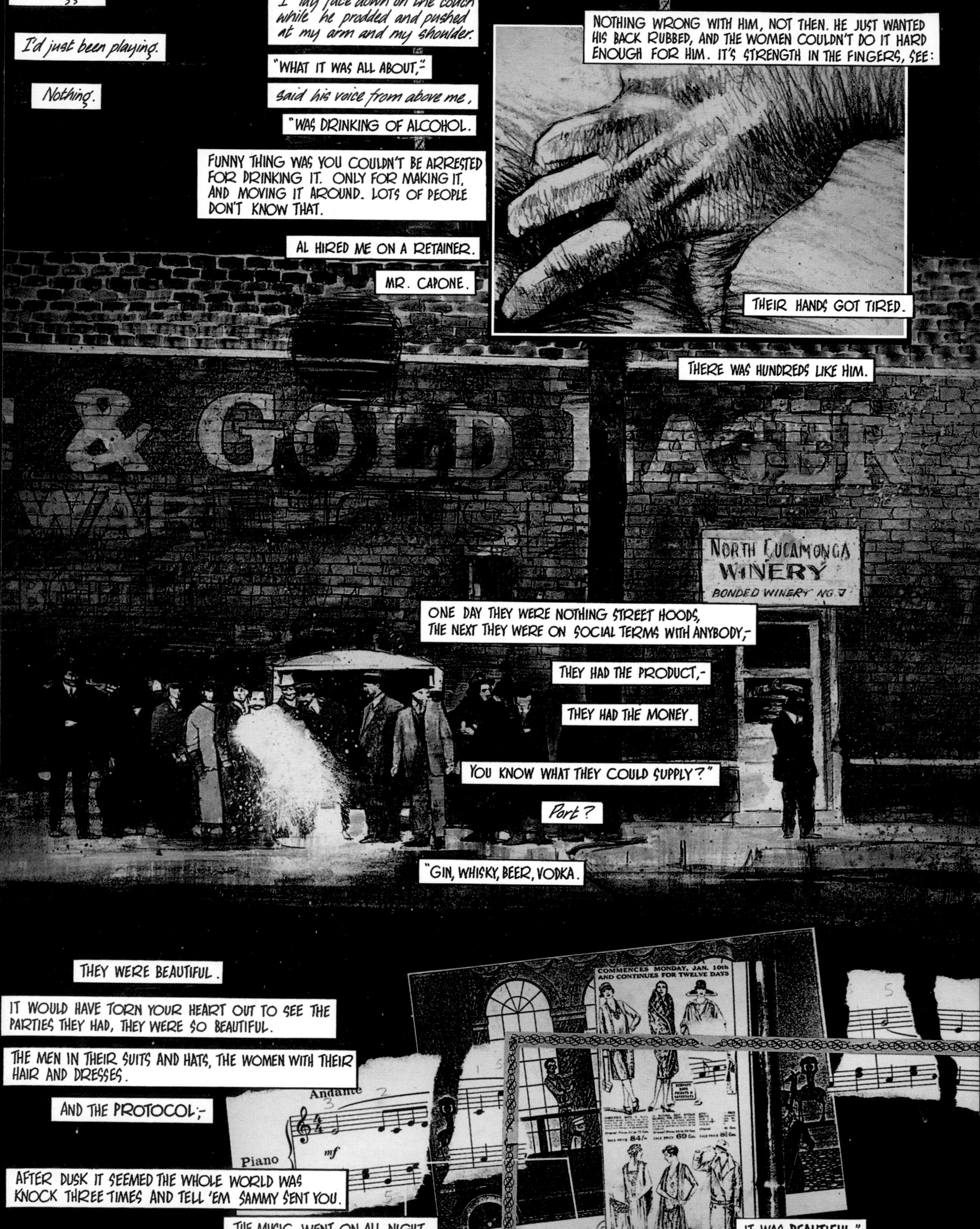
I'd just been playing.
Nothing.
I lay face down on the couch while he prodded and pushed at my arm and my shoulder.
"WHAT IT WAS ALL ABOUT,"
said his voice from above me.
"WAS DRINKING OF ALCOHOL.
FUNNY THING WAS YOU COULDN'T BE ARRESTED FOR DRINKING IT. ONLY FOR MAKING IT, AND MOVING IT AROUND. LOTS OF PEOPLE DON'T KNOW THAT.
AL HIRED ME ON A RETAINER.
MR. CAPONE.
NOTHING WRONG WITH HIM, NOT THEN. HE JUST WANTED HIS BACK RUBBED, AND THE WOMEN COULDN'T DO IT HARD ENOUGH FOR HIM. IT'S STRENGTH IN THE FINGERS, SEE:
THEIR HANDS GOT TIRED.
THERE WAS HUNDREDS LIKE HIM.
& GOLD LAGER
NORTH CUCAMONGA WINERY
BONDED WINERY NO. 7
ONE DAY THEY WERE NOTHING STREET HOODS, THE NEXT THEY WERE ON SOCIAL TERMS WITH ANYBODY,-
THEY HAD THE PRODUCT,-
THEY HAD THE MONEY.
YOU KNOW WHAT THEY COULD SUPPLY?"
Port?
"GIN, WHISKY, BEER, VODKA.
THEY WERE BEAUTIFUL.
IT WOULD HAVE TORN YOUR HEART OUT TO SEE THE PARTIES THEY HAD, THEY WERE SO BEAUTIFUL.
THE MEN IN THEIR SUITS AND HATS, THE WOMEN WITH THEIR HAIR AND DRESSES.
AND THE PROTOCOL;-
AFTER DUSK IT SEEMED THE WHOLE WORLD WAS KNOCK THREE TIMES AND TELL 'EM SAMMY SENT YOU.
COMMENCES MONDAY, JAN. 10th AND CONTINUES FOR TWELVE DAYS
Andante
Piano

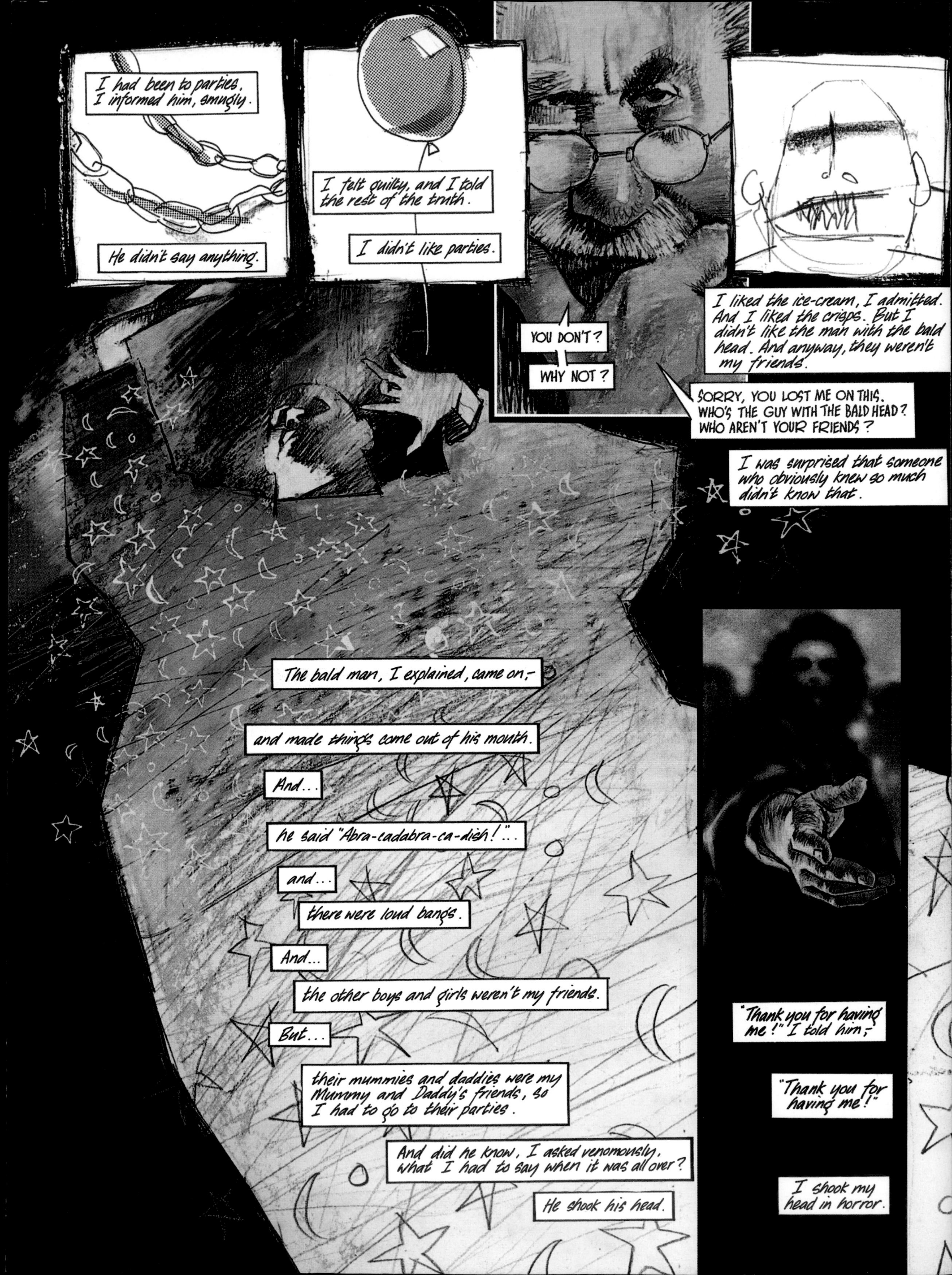

I had been to parties, I informed him, smugly.
He didn't say anything.
I felt guilty, and I told the rest of the truth.
I didn't like parties.
YOU DON'T?
WHY NOT?
I liked the ice-cream, I admitted. And I liked the crisps. But I didn't like the man with the bald head. And anyway, they weren't my friends.
SORRY, YOU LOST ME ON THIS. WHO'S THE GUY WITH THE BALD HEAD? WHO AREN'T YOUR FRIENDS?
I was surprised that someone who obviously knew so much didn't know that.
The bald man, I explained, came on,-
and made things come out of his mouth.
And...
he said "Abra-cadabra-ca-dish!"...
and...
there were loud bangs.
And...
the other boys and girls weren't my friends.
But...
their mummies and daddies were my Mummy and Daddy's friends, so I had to go to their parties.
And did he know, I asked venomously, what I had to say when it was all over?
He shook his head.
"Thank you for having me!" I told him,-
"Thank you for having me!"
I shook my head in horror.

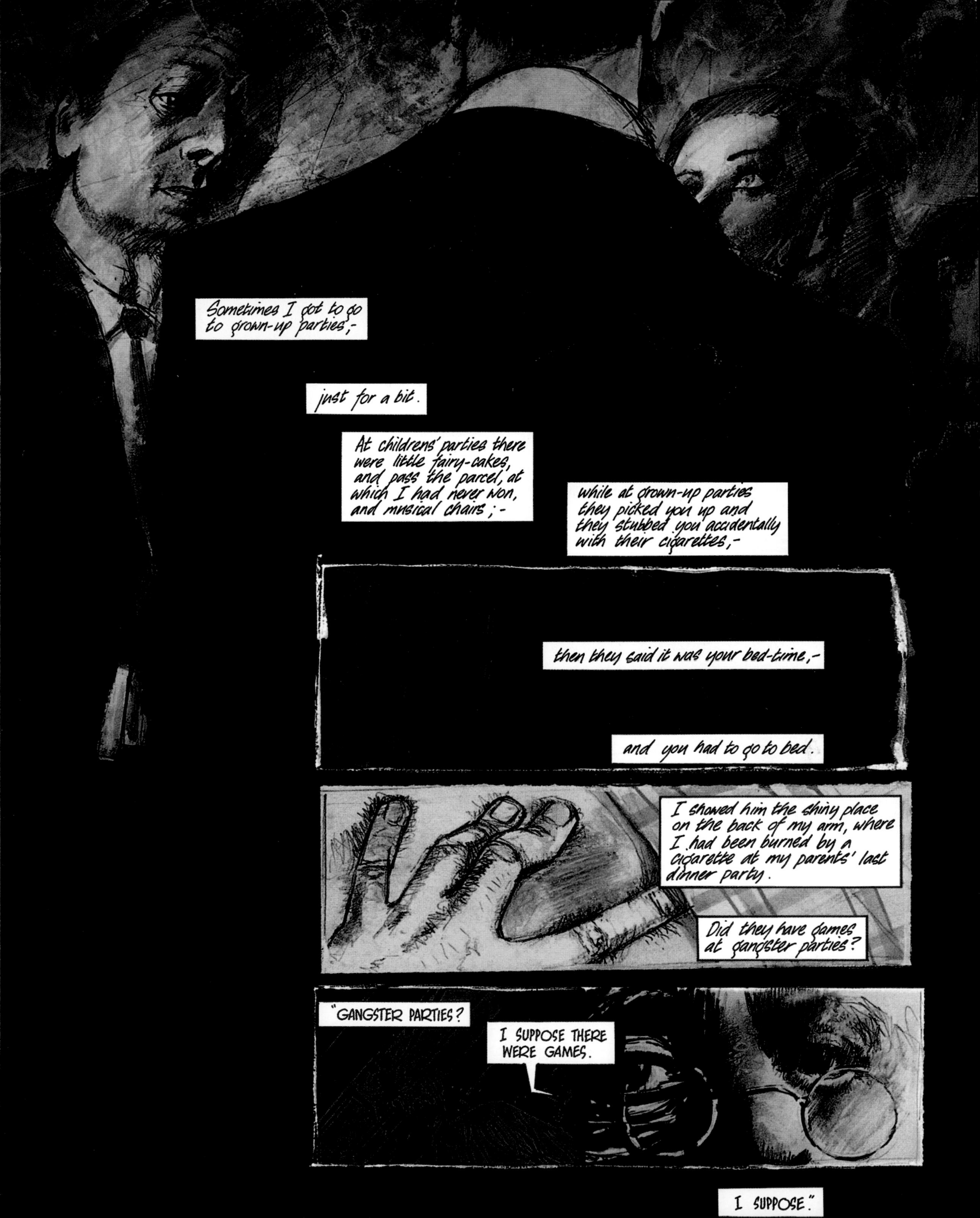
Sometimes I got to go to grown-up parties;-
just for a bit.
At childrens' parties there were little fairy-cakes, and pass the parcel, at which I had never won, and musical chairs;-
while at grown-up parties they picked you up and they stubbed you accidentally with their cigarettes;-
then they said it was your bed-time,-
and you had to go to bed.
I showed him the shiny place on the back of my arm, where I had been burned by a cigarette at my parents' last dinner party.
Did they have games at gangster parties?
"GANGSTER PARTIES?
I SUPPOSE THERE WERE GAMES.
I SUPPOSE."

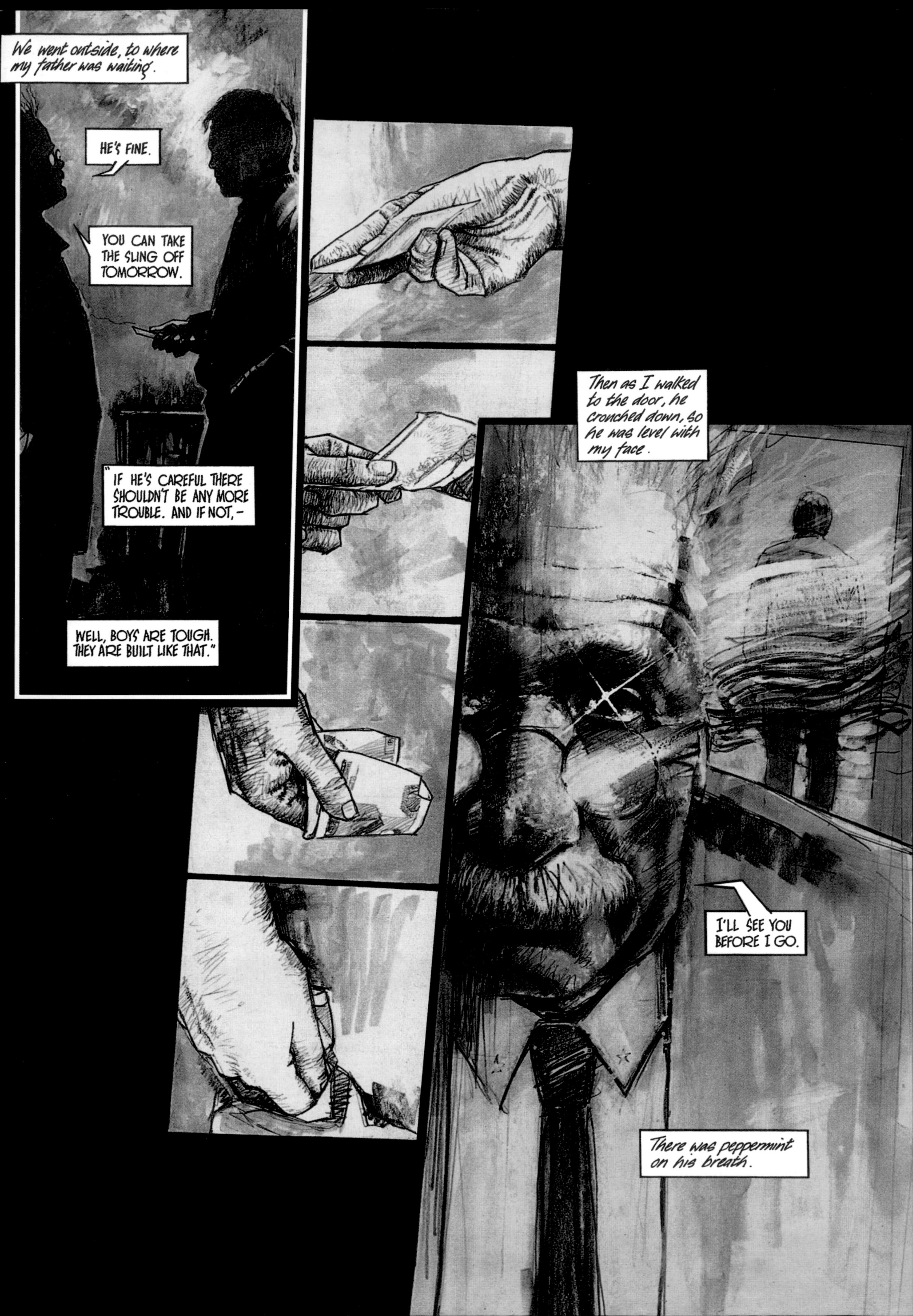
We went outside, to where my father was waiting.
HE'S FINE.
YOU CAN TAKE THE SLING OFF TOMORROW.
"IF HE'S CAREFUL THERE SHOULDN'T BE ANY MORE TROUBLE. AND IF NOT,-
WELL, BOYS ARE TOUGH. THEY ARE BUILT LIKE THAT."
Then as I walked to the door, he crouched down, so he was level with my face.
I'LL SEE YOU BEFORE I GO.
There was peppermint on his breath.

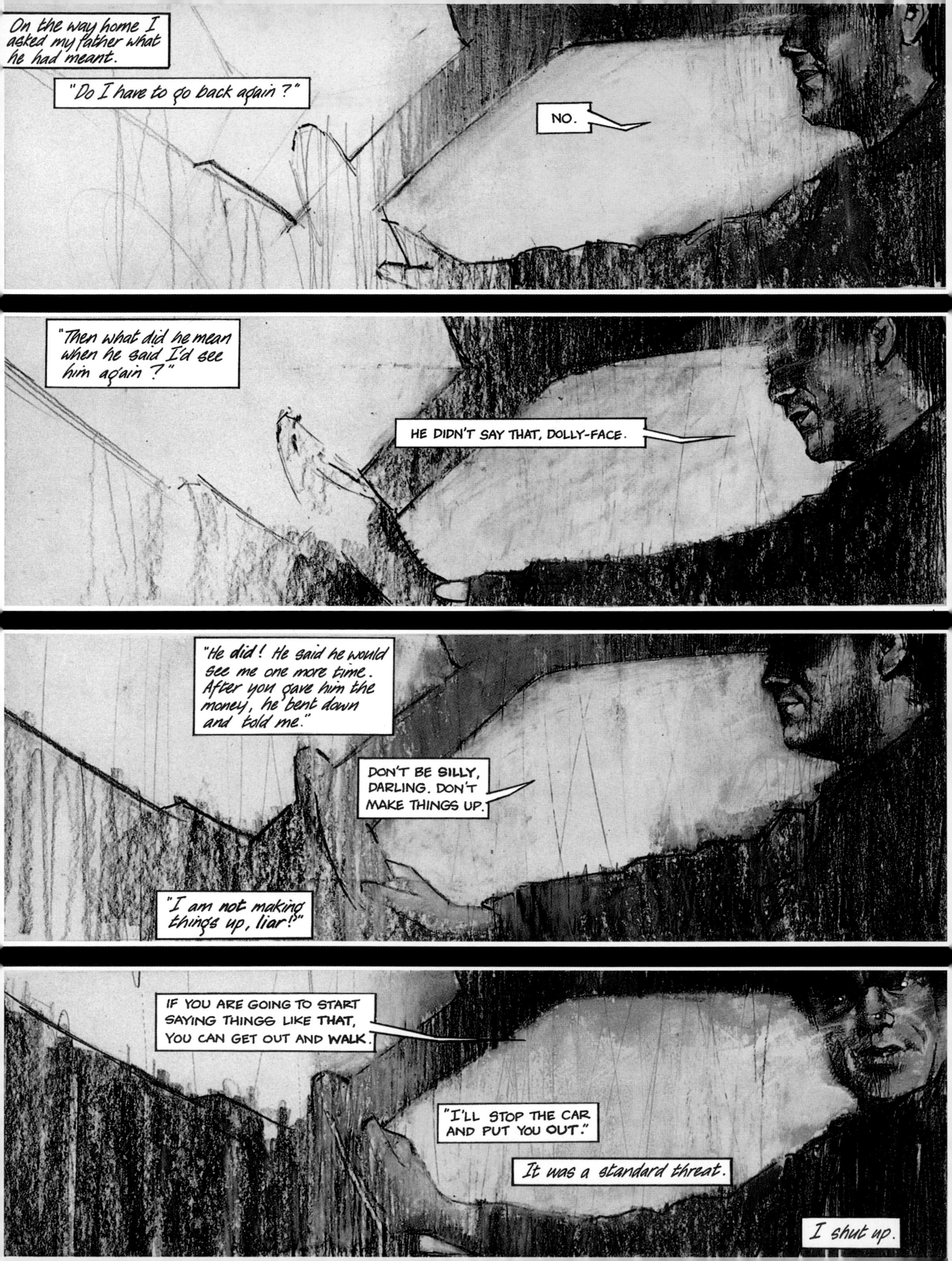
On the way home I asked my father what he had meant.
"Do I have to go back again?"
NO.
"Then what did he mean when he said I'd see him again?"
HE DIDN'T SAY THAT, DOLLY-FACE.
"He did! He said he would see me one more time. After you gave him the money, he bent down and told me."
DON'T BE SILLY, DARLING. DON'T MAKE THINGS UP.
"I am not making things up, liar!"
IF YOU ARE GOING TO START SAYING THINGS LIKE THAT, YOU CAN GET OUT AND WALK.
"I'LL STOP THE CAR AND PUT YOU OUT."
It was a standard threat.
I shut up.

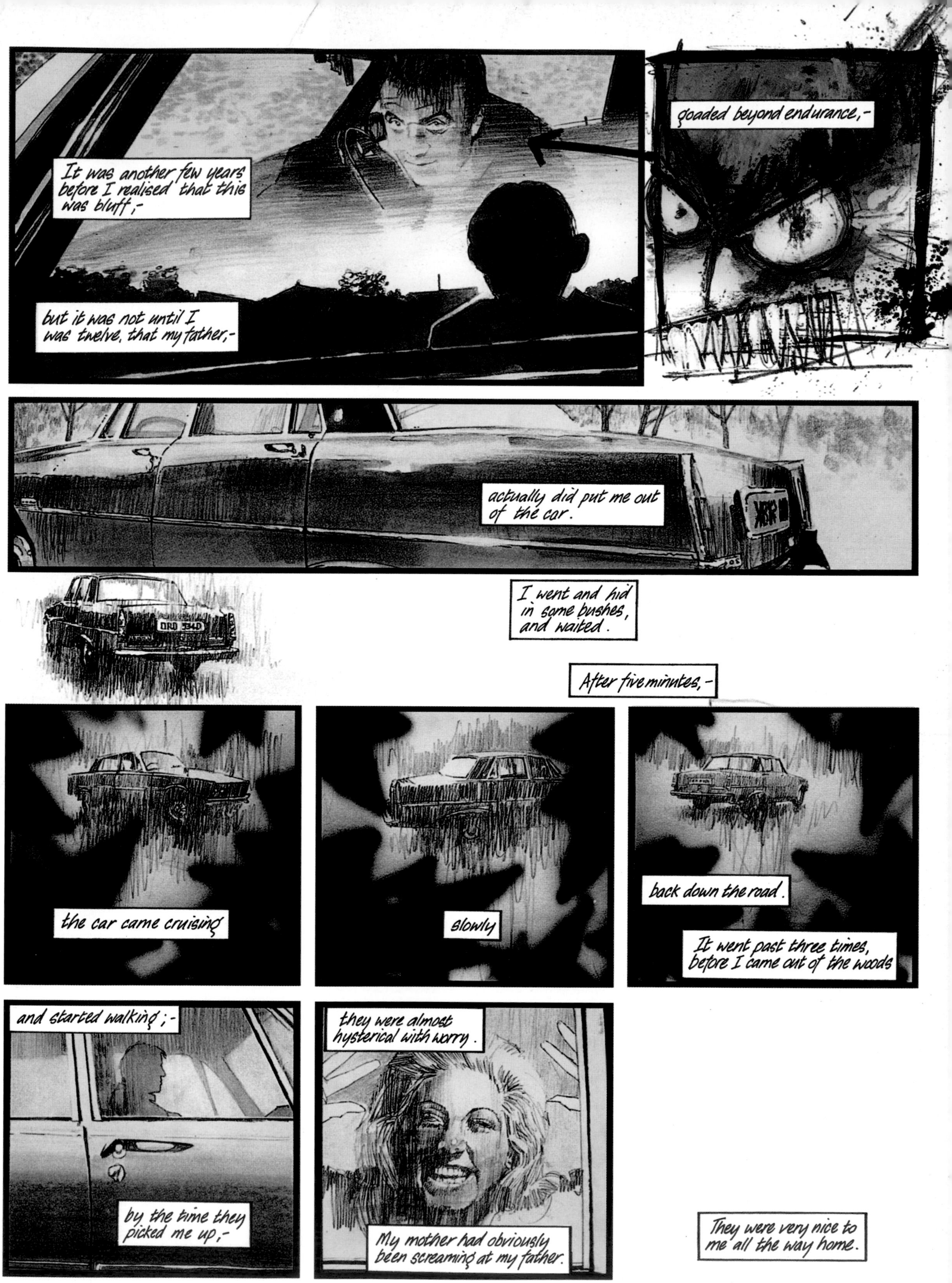
It was another few years before I realised that this was bluff;-
but it was not until I was twelve, that my father,-
goaded beyond endurance,-
actually did put me out of the car.
I went and hid in some bushes, and waited.
After five minutes,-
the car came cruising
slowly
back down the road.
It went past three times, before I came out of the woods
and started walking;-
by the time they picked me up,-
they were almost hysterical with worry.
My mother had obviously been screaming at my father.
They were very nice to me all the way home.

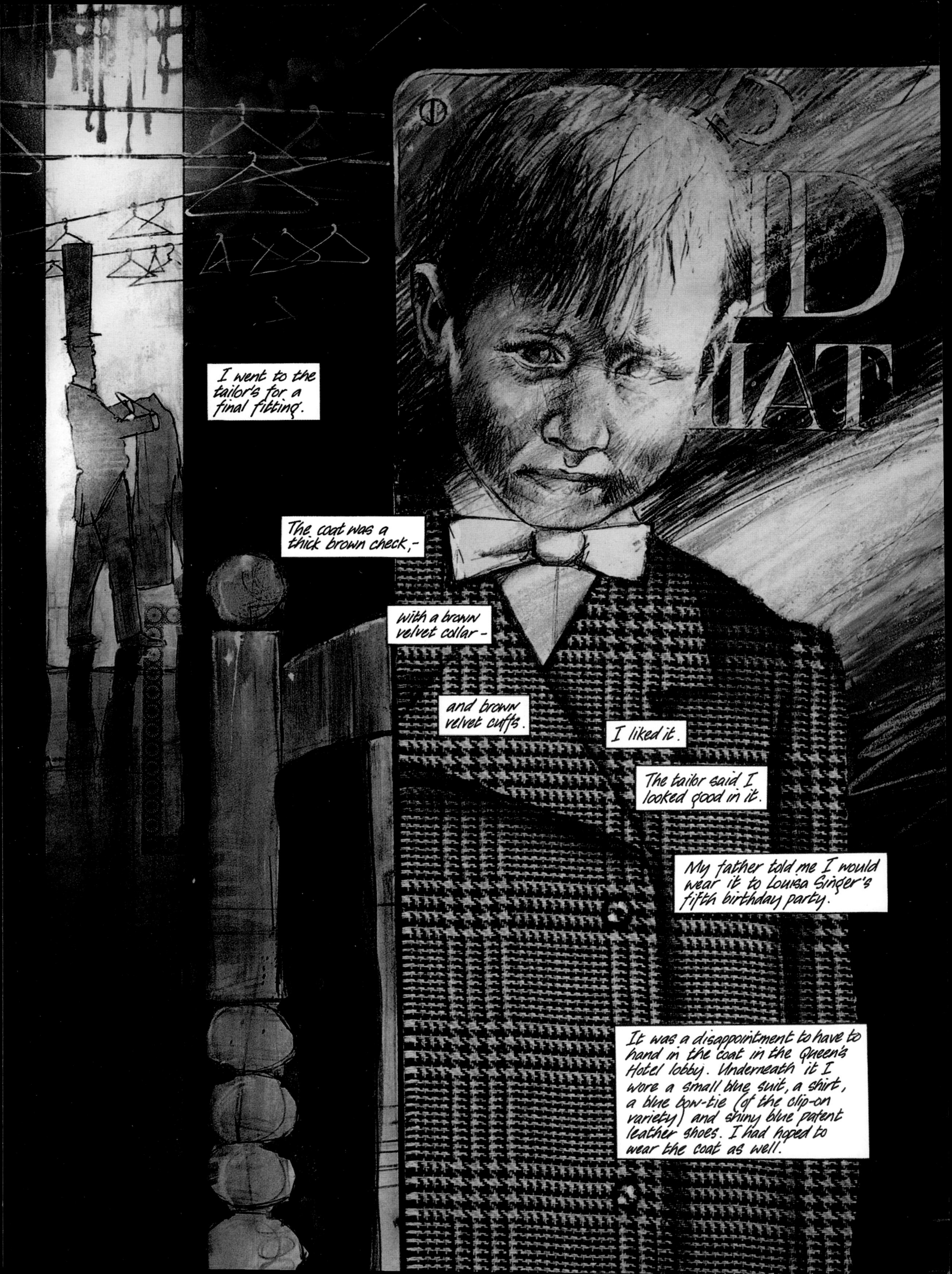

I went to the tailor's for a final fitting.
The coat was a thick brown check,-
with a brown velvet collar-
and brown velvet cuffs.
I liked it.
The tailor said I looked good in it.
My father told me I would wear it to Louisa Singer's fifth birthday party.
It was a disappointment to have to hand in the coat in the Queen's Hotel lobby. Underneath it I wore a small blue suit, a shirt, a blue bow-tie (of the clip-on variety) and shiny blue patent leather shoes. I had hoped to wear the coat as well.

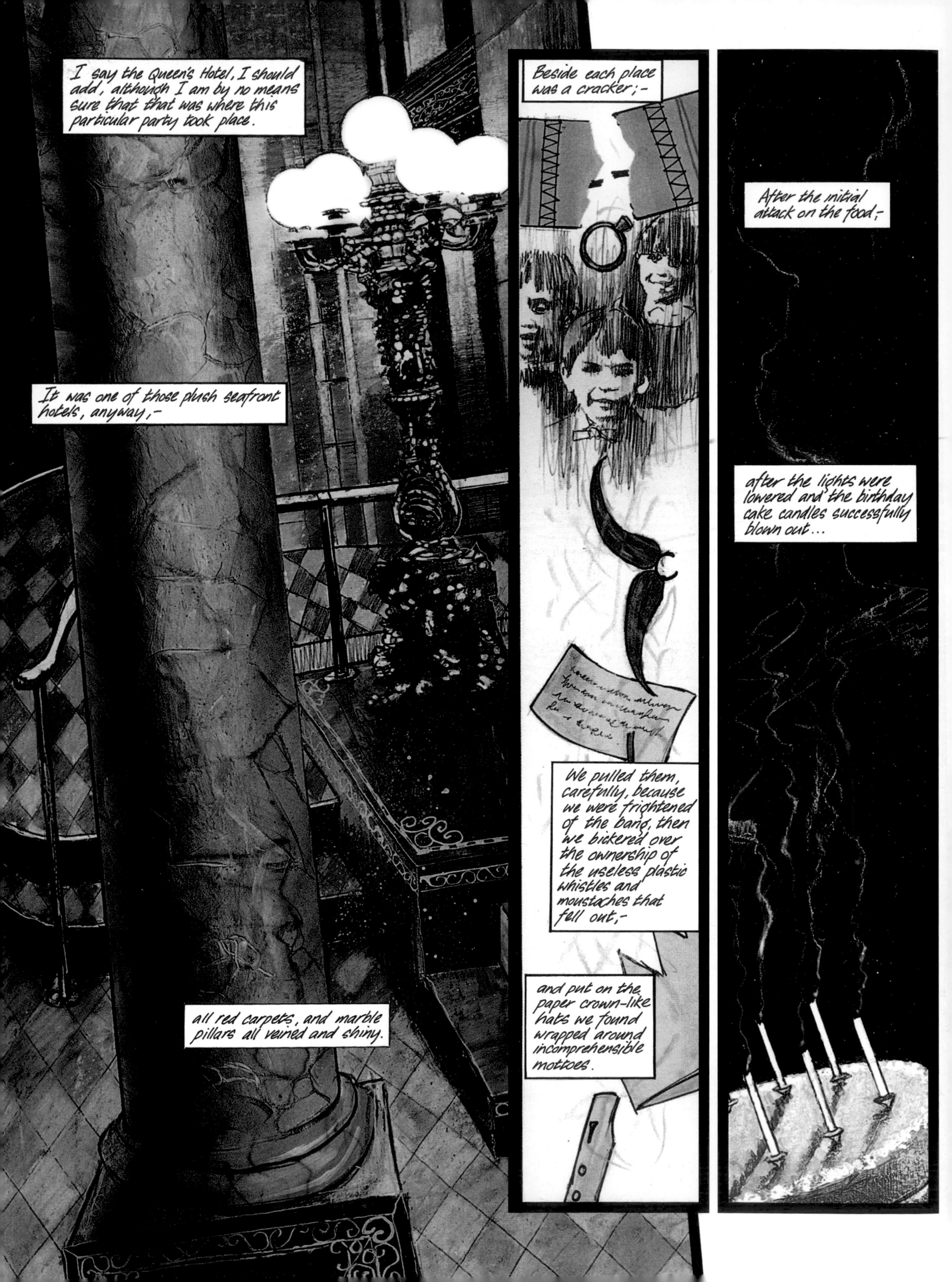
I say the Queen's Hotel, I should add, although I am by no means sure that that was where this particular party took place.
It was one of those plush seafront hotels, anyway,-
all red carpets, and marble pillars all veined and shiny.
Beside each place was a cracker;-
We pulled them, carefully, because we were frightened of the bang, then we bickered over the ownership of the useless plastic whistles and moustaches that fell out,-
and put on the paper crown-like hats we found wrapped around incomprehensible mottoes.
After the initial attack on the food,-
after the lights were lowered and the birthday cake candles successfully blown out...

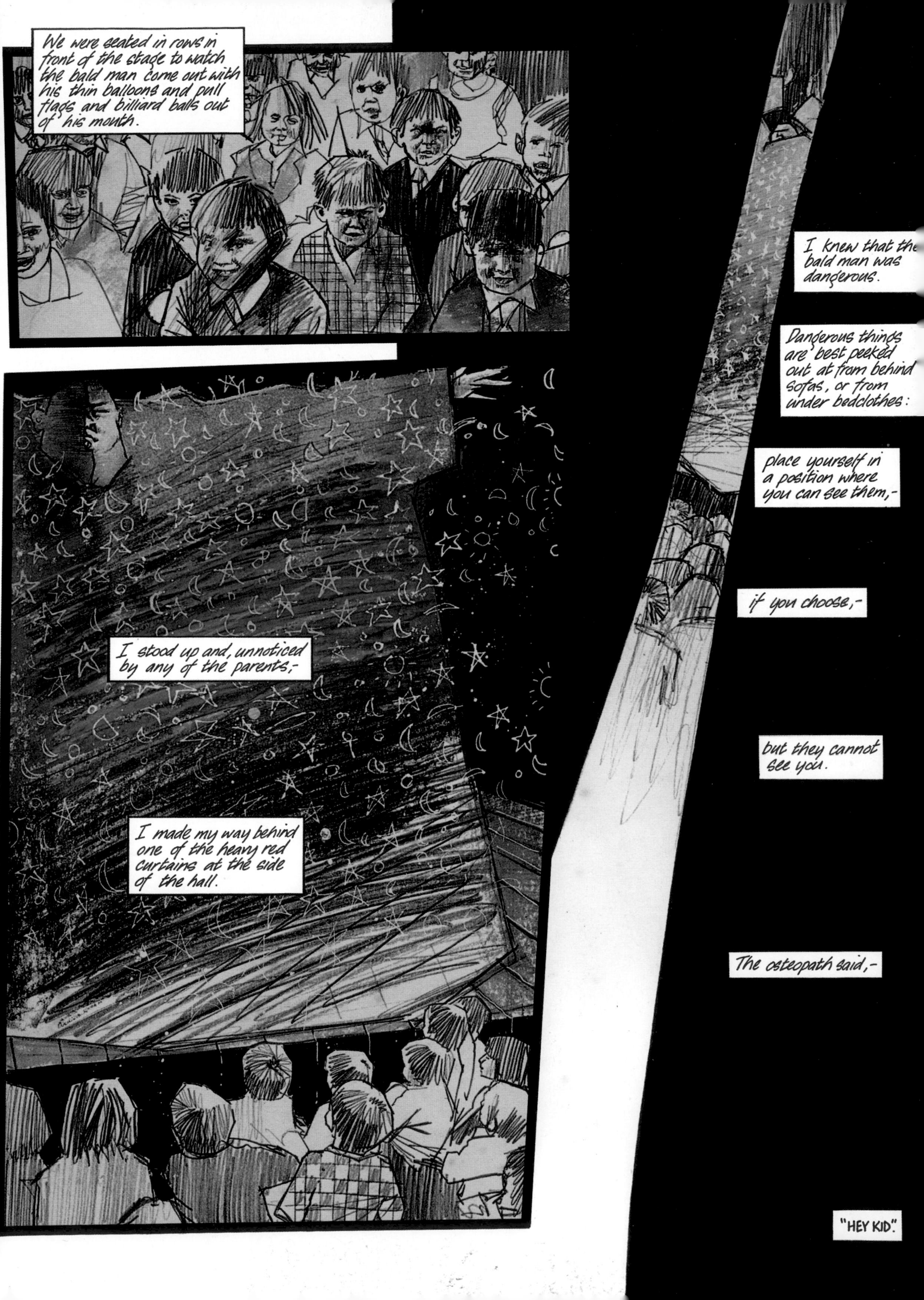
We were seated in rows in front of the stage to watch the bald man come out with his thin balloons and pull flags and billiard balls out of his mouth.
I stood up and, unnoticed by any of the parents,-
I made my way behind one of the heavy red curtains at the side of the hall.
I knew that the bald man was dangerous.
Dangerous things are best peeked out at from behind sofas, or from under bedclothes:
place yourself in a position where you can see them,-
if you choose,-
but they cannot see you.
The osteopath said,-
"HEY KID".

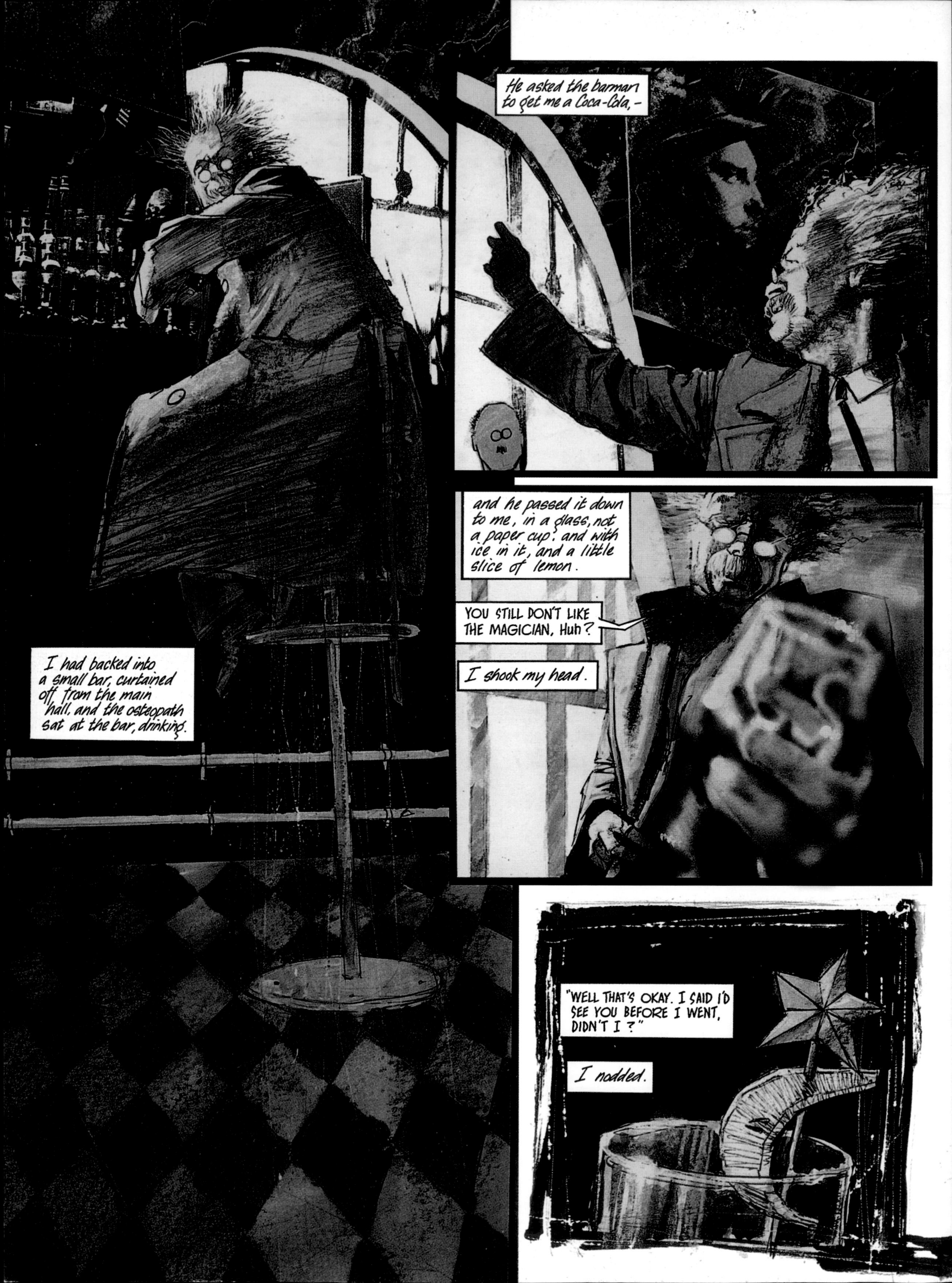
I had backed into a small bar, curtained off from the main hall, and the osteopath sat at the bar, drinking.
He asked the barman to get me a Coca-Cola, -
and he passed it down to me, in a glass, not a paper cup: and with ice in it, and a little slice of lemon.
YOU STILL DON'T LIKE THE MAGICIAN, Huh?
I shook my head.
"WELL THAT'S OKAY. I SAID I'D SEE YOU BEFORE I WENT, DIDN'T I?"
I nodded.

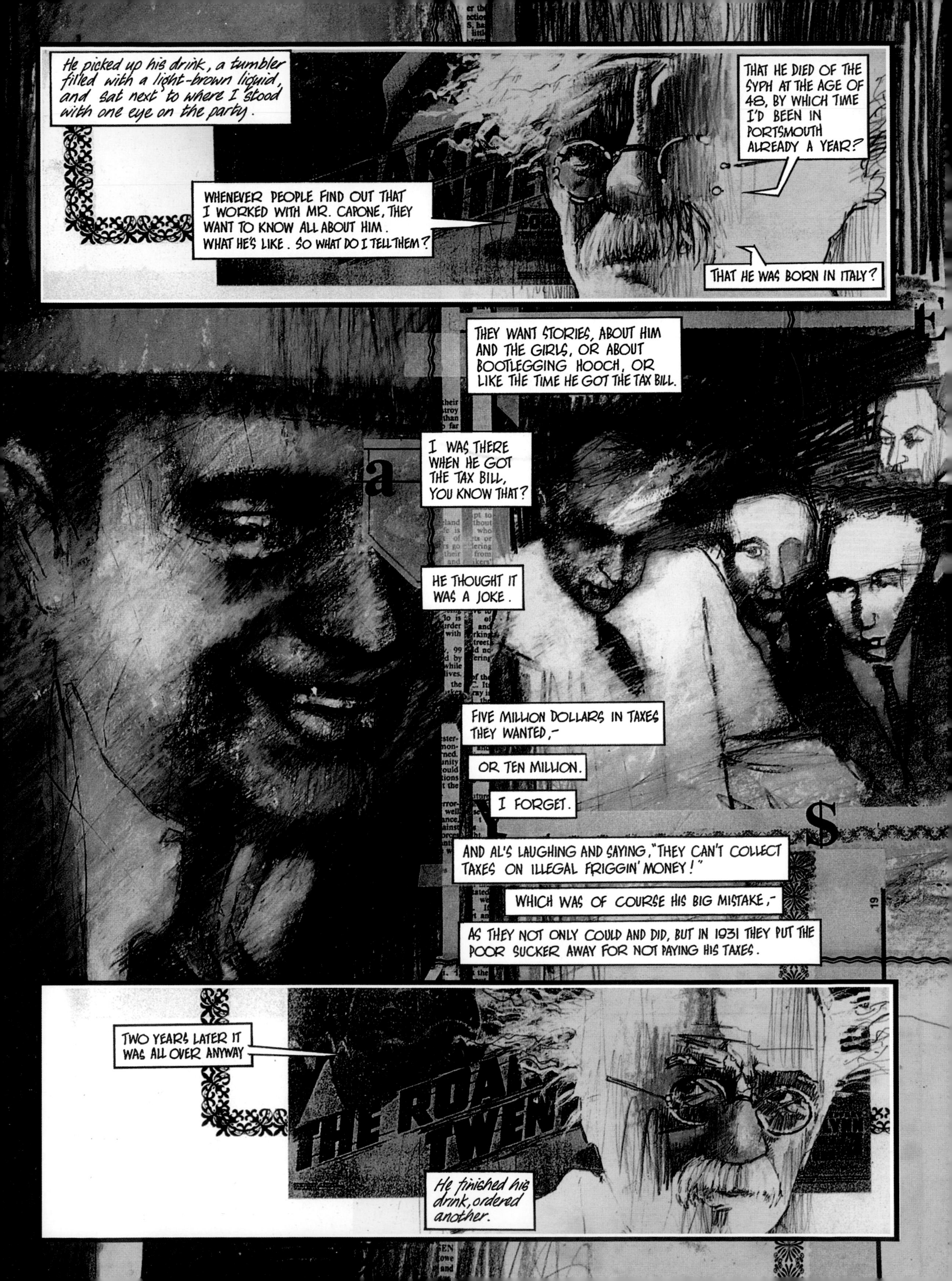
He picked up his drink, a tumbler filled with a light-brown liquid, and sat next to where I stood with one eye on the party.
WHENEVER PEOPLE FIND OUT THAT I WORKED WITH MR. CAPONE, THEY WANT TO KNOW ALL ABOUT HIM. WHAT HE'S LIKE. SO WHAT DO I TELL THEM?
THAT HE DIED OF THE SYPH AT THE AGE OF 48, BY WHICH TIME I'D BEEN IN PORTSMOUTH ALREADY A YEAR?
THAT HE WAS BORN IN ITALY?
THEY WANT STORIES, ABOUT HIM AND THE GIRLS, OR ABOUT BOOTLEGGING HOOCH, OR LIKE THE TIME HE GOT THE TAX BILL.
I WAS THERE WHEN HE GOT THE TAX BILL, YOU KNOW THAT?
HE THOUGHT IT WAS A JOKE.
FIVE MILLION DOLLARS IN TAXES THEY WANTED,-
OR TEN MILLION.
I FORGET.
AND AL'S LAUGHING AND SAYING, "THEY CAN'T COLLECT TAXES ON ILLEGAL FRIGGIN' MONEY!"
WHICH WAS OF COURSE HIS BIG MISTAKE,-
AS THEY NOT ONLY COULD AND DID, BUT IN 1931 THEY PUT THE POOR SUCKER AWAY FOR NOT PAYING HIS TAXES.
TWO YEARS LATER IT WAS ALL OVER ANYWAY
THE ROA
TWEN
He finished his drink, ordered another.

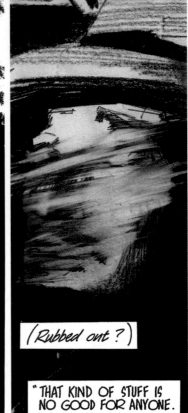

"HE WAS A BASTARD, –

SORRY, LANGUAGE, –

HE WAS AN OKAY BASTARD, THOUGH.

LIKE WHEN O'BANION –

STARTED SAYING THAT STUFF ABOUT SICILIANS, AL AND JOHNNY TORRIO HAD TO HAVE HIM RUBBED OUT."

(Rubbed ont ?)

"THAT KIND OF STUFF IS NO GOOD FOR ANYONE.

BUT YOU KNOW WHAT THEY GAVE HIM ?

YOU KNOW ?"

I shook my head.

"THEY GAVE HIM A SILVER COFFIN.

THEY WALKED BEHIND HIS COFFIN, WITH THE IRISHERS, AND AL HIMSELF PAID FOR FIVE THOUSAND DOLLARS' WORTH OF FLOWERS !

AND AFTER THAT, IF ANYBODY SAID ANYTHING NASTY ABOUT THE SICILIANS, –

THEY SAID IT QUIET, –

AND THEY SAID IT WHERE NOBODY COULD HEAR THEM TALKING."

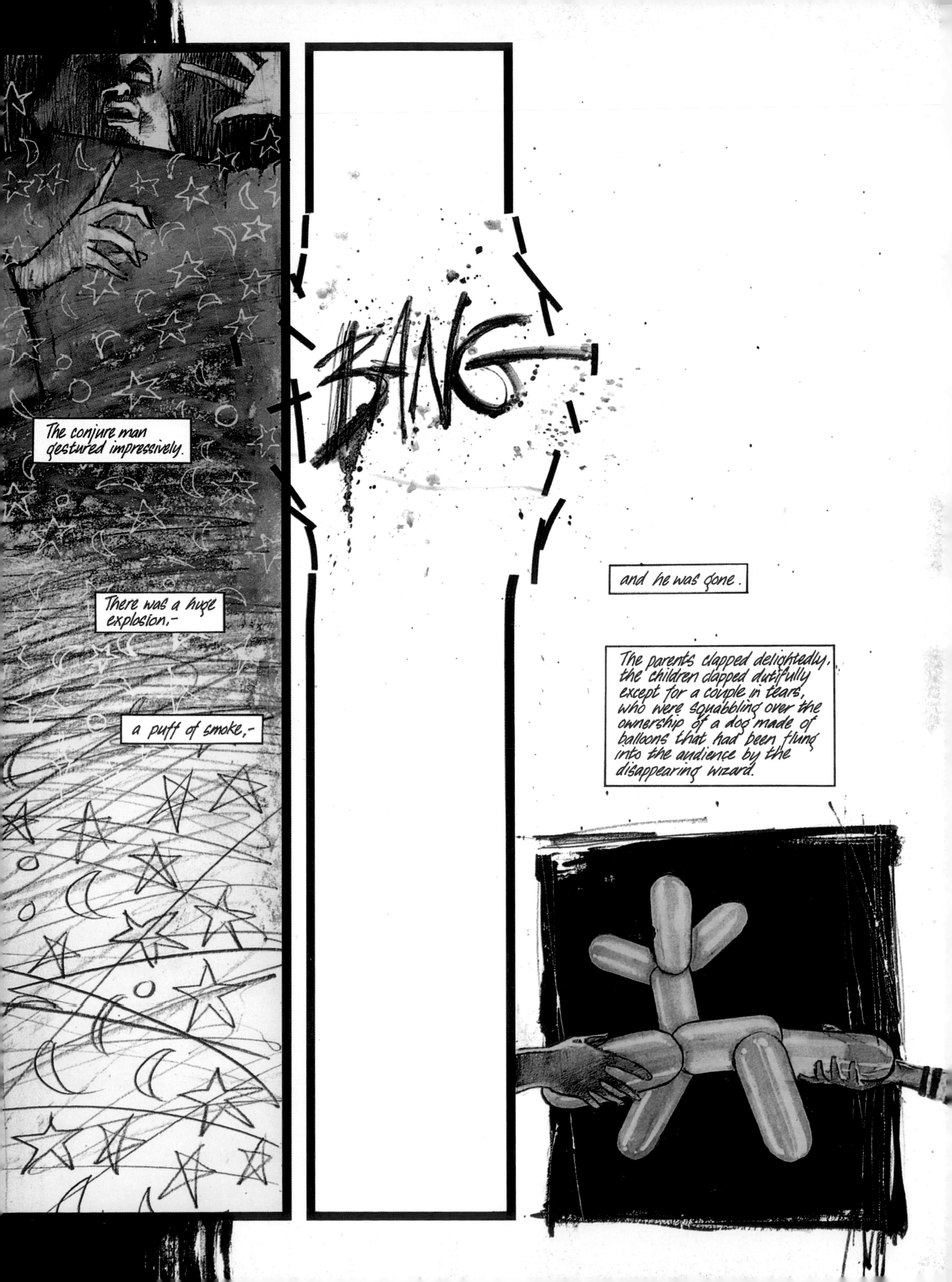
The conjure man gestured impressively.
There was a huge explosion,-
a puff of smoke,-
BANG
and he was gone.
The parents clapped delightedly, the children clapped dutifully except for a couple in tears, who were squabbling over the ownership of a dog made of balloons that had been flung into the audience by the disappearing wizard.

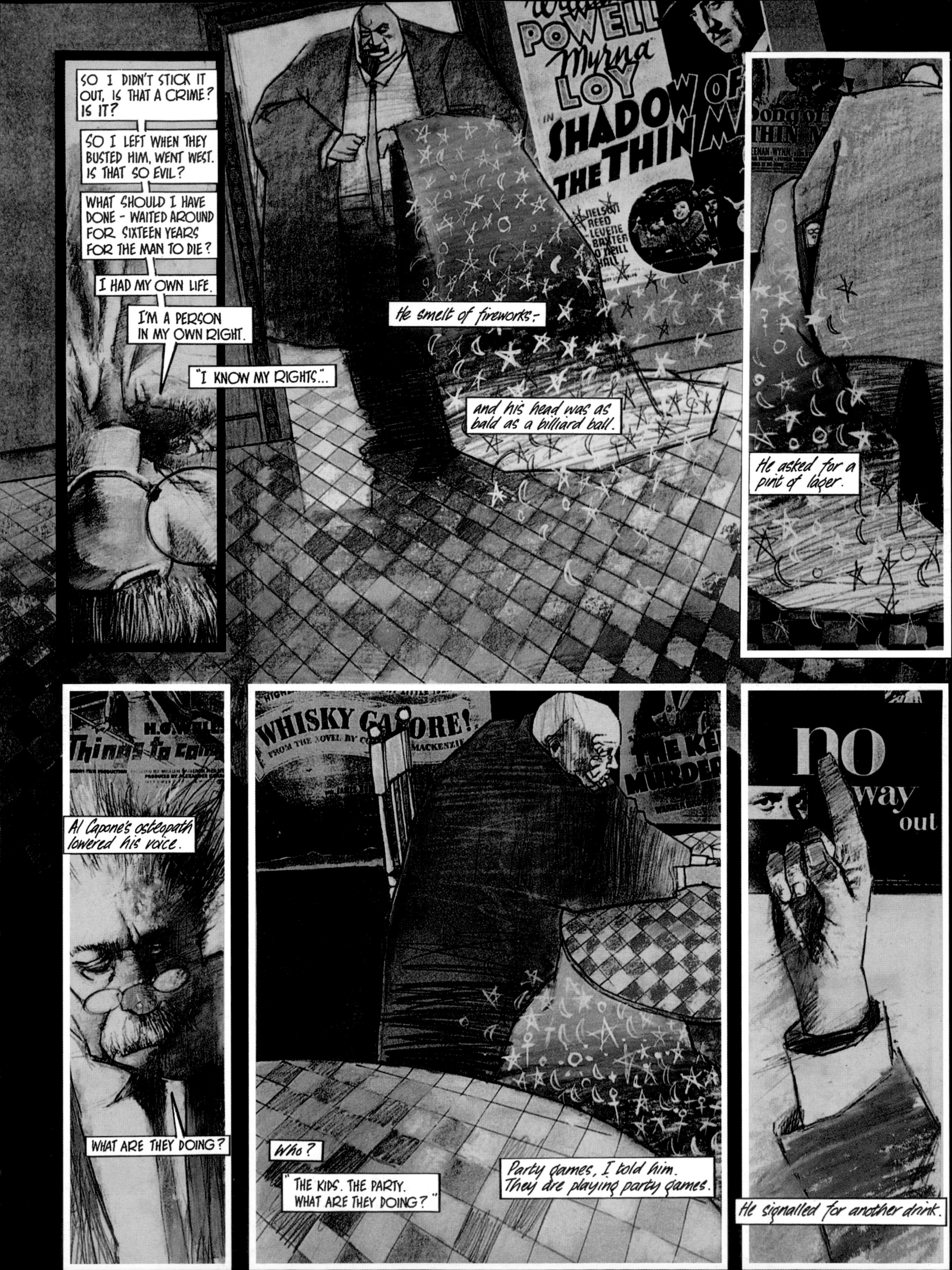

SO I DIDN'T STICK IT OUT, IS THAT A CRIME? IS IT?
SO I LEFT WHEN THEY BUSTED HIM, WENT WEST. IS THAT SO EVIL?
WHAT SHOULD I HAVE DONE - WAITED AROUND FOR SIXTEEN YEARS FOR THE MAN TO DIE?
I HAD MY OWN LIFE.
I'M A PERSON IN MY OWN RIGHT.
"I KNOW MY RIGHTS."
POWELL
Myrna LOY
IN SHADOW OF
THE THIN
He smelt of fireworks:-
and his head was as bald as a billiard ball.
He asked for a pint of lager.
Al Capone's osteopath lowered his voice.
WHAT ARE THEY DOING?
Who?
"THE KIDS. THE PARTY. WHAT ARE THEY DOING?"
Party games, I told him. They are playing party games.
no
way
out
He signalled for another drink.

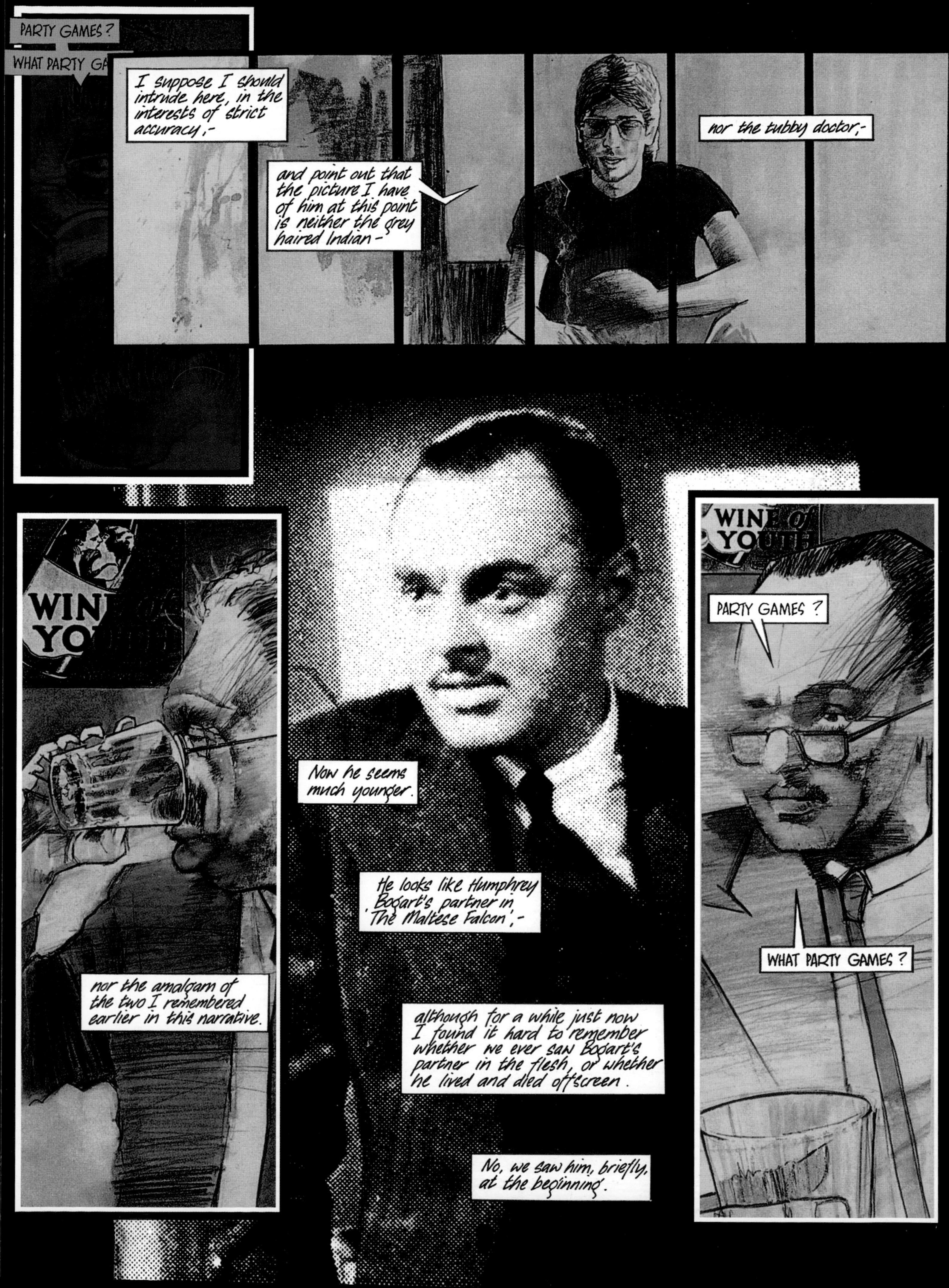
PARTY GAMES?
WHAT PARTY GA
I suppose I should intrude here, in the interests of strict accuracy,-
and point out that the picture I have of him at this point is neither the grey haired Indian-
nor the tubby doctor,-
nor the amalgam of the two I remembered earlier in this narrative.
Now he seems much younger.
He looks like Humphrey Bogart's partner in 'The Maltese Falcon',-
although for a while just now I found it hard to remember whether we ever saw Bogart's partner in the flesh, or whether he lived and died offscreen.
No, we saw him, briefly, at the beginning.
WINE of YOUTH
PARTY GAMES?
WHAT PARTY GAMES?

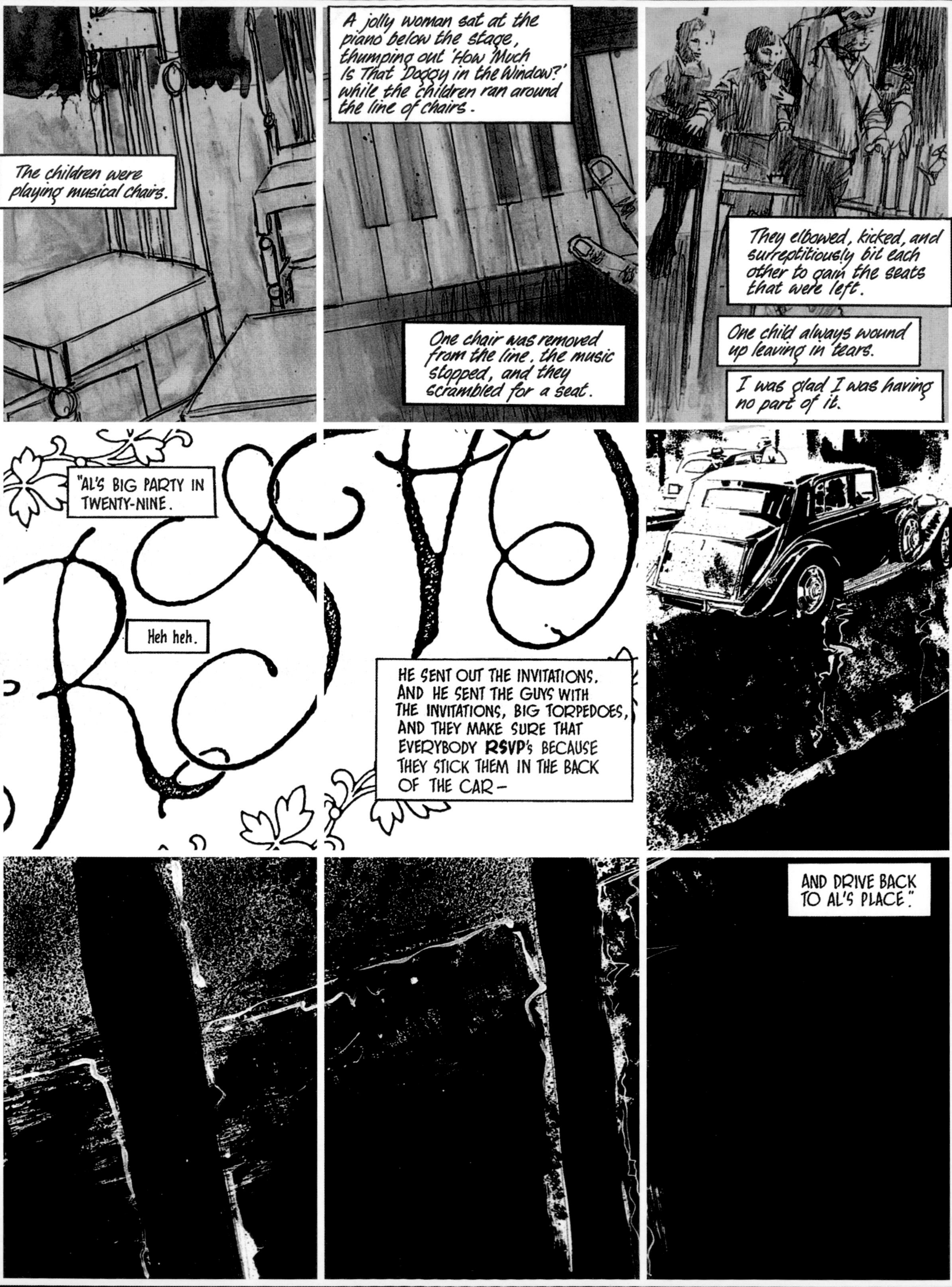
The children were playing musical chairs.
A jolly woman sat at the piano below the stage, thumping out 'How Much Is That Doggy in the Window?' while the children ran around the line of chairs.
One chair was removed from the line. the music stopped, and they scrambled for a seat.
They elbowed, kicked, and surreptitiously bit each other to gain the seats that were left.
One child always wound up leaving in tears.
I was glad I was having no part of it.
"AL'S BIG PARTY IN TWENTY-NINE.
Heh heh.
HE SENT OUT THE INVITATIONS. AND HE SENT THE GUYS WITH THE INVITATIONS, BIG TORPEDOES, AND THEY MAKE SURE THAT EVERYBODY RSVP's BECAUSE THEY STICK THEM IN THE BACK OF THE CAR–
AND DRIVE BACK TO AL'S PLACE."

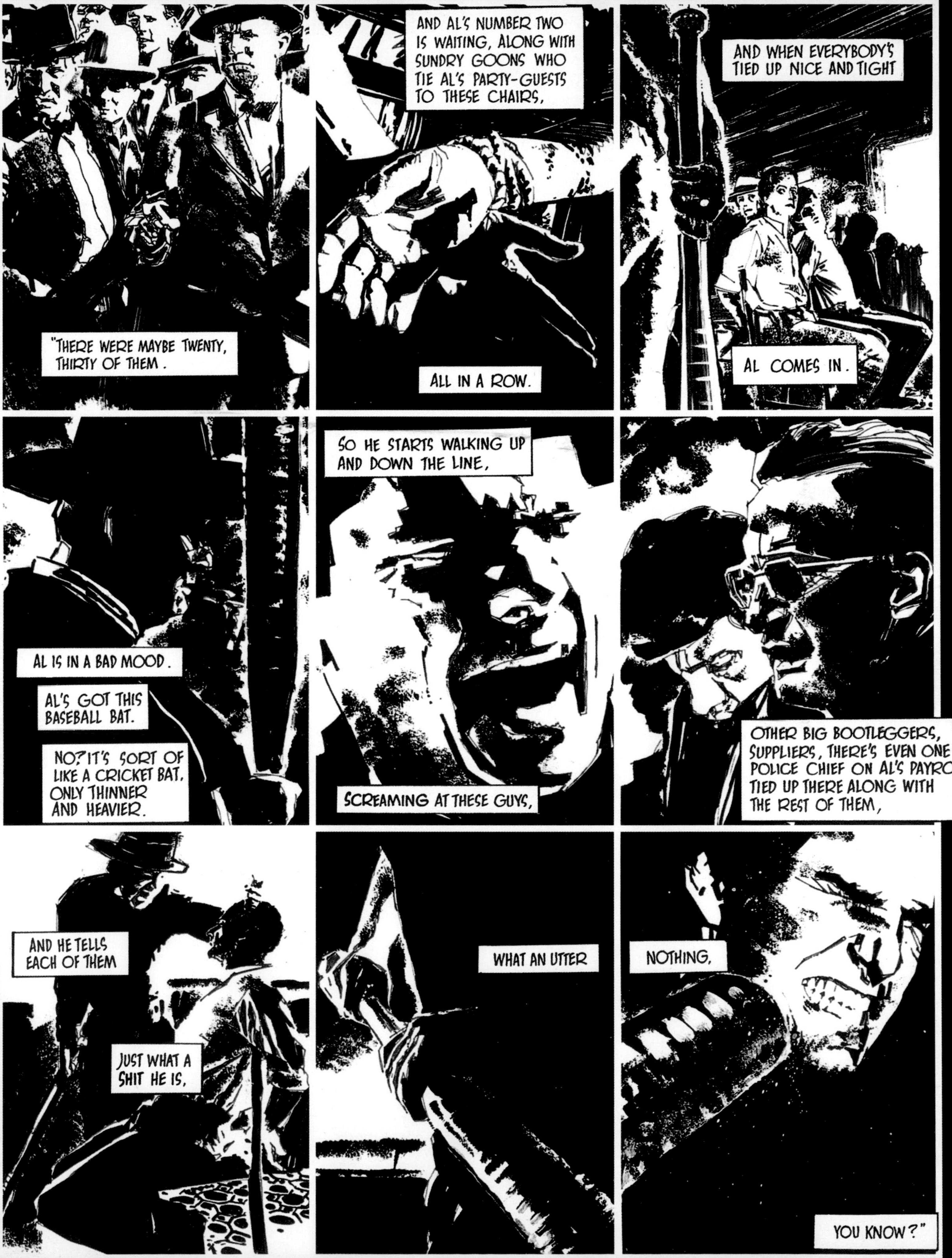
"THERE WERE MAYBE TWENTY, THIRTY OF THEM.
AND AL'S NUMBER TWO IS WAITING, ALONG WITH SUNDRY GOONS WHO TIE AL'S PARTY-GUESTS TO THESE CHAIRS,
ALL IN A ROW.
AND WHEN EVERYBODY'S TIED UP NICE AND TIGHT
AL COMES IN.
AL IS IN A BAD MOOD.
AL'S GOT THIS BASEBALL BAT.
NO? IT'S SORT OF LIKE A CRICKET BAT, ONLY THINNER AND HEAVIER.
SO HE STARTS WALKING UP AND DOWN THE LINE,
SCREAMING AT THESE GUYS,
OTHER BIG BOOTLEGGERS, SUPPLIERS, THERE'S EVEN ONE POLICE CHIEF ON AL'S PAYROLL TIED UP THERE ALONG WITH THE REST OF THEM,
AND HE TELLS EACH OF THEM
JUST WHAT A SHIT HE IS,
WHAT AN UTTER
NOTHING,
YOU KNOW?"

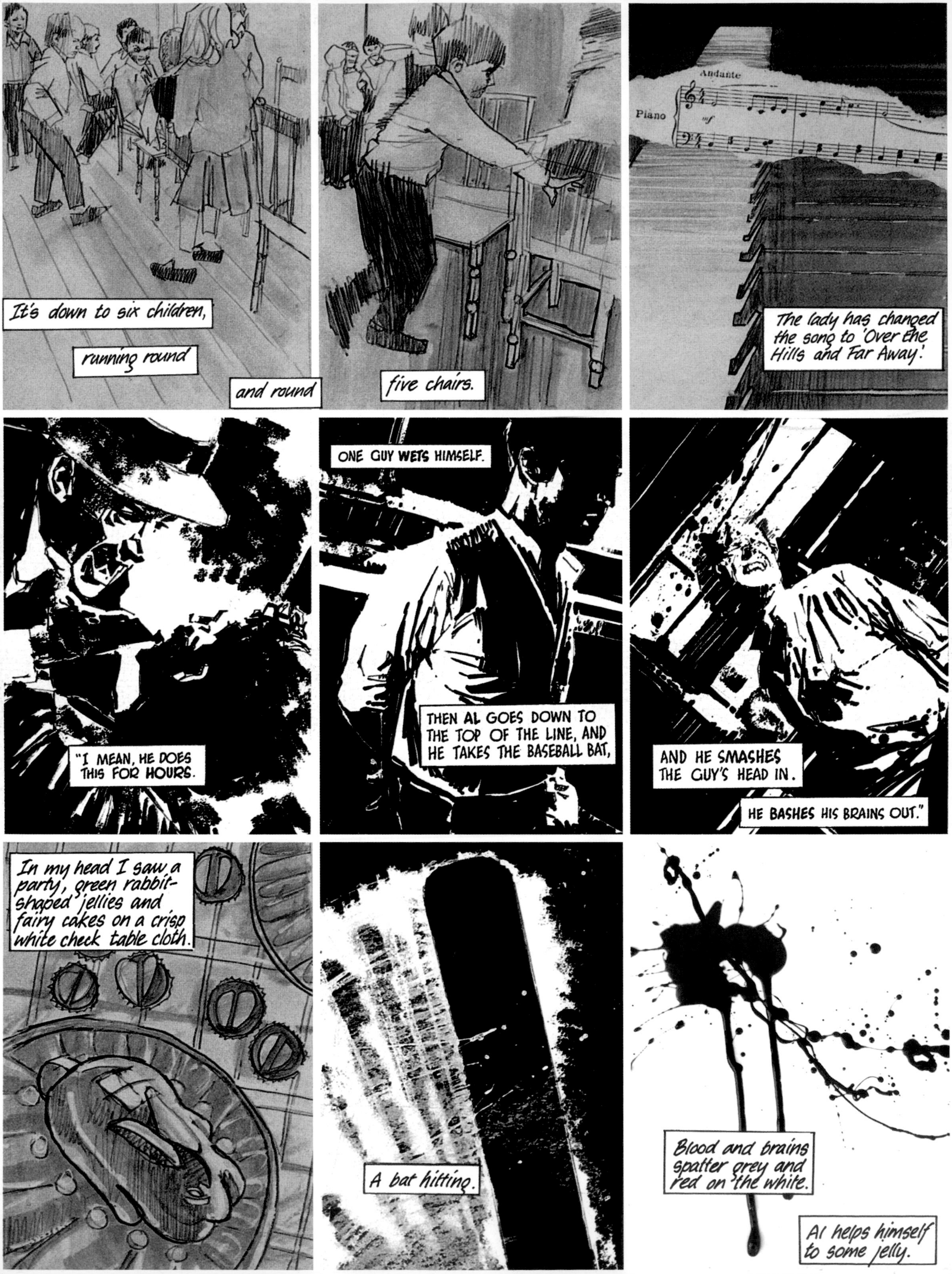

It's down to six children,
running round
and round
five chairs.
Andante
Piano
mf
The lady has changed the song to 'Over the Hills and Far Away'.
"I MEAN, HE DOES THIS FOR HOURS.
ONE GUY WETS HIMSELF.
THEN AL GOES DOWN TO THE TOP OF THE LINE, AND HE TAKES THE BASEBALL BAT,
AND HE SMASHES THE GUY'S HEAD IN.
HE BASHES HIS BRAINS OUT."
In my head I saw a party, green rabbit-shaped jellies and fairy cakes on a crisp white check table cloth.
A bat hitting.
Blood and brains spatter grey and red on the white.
Al helps himself to some jelly.

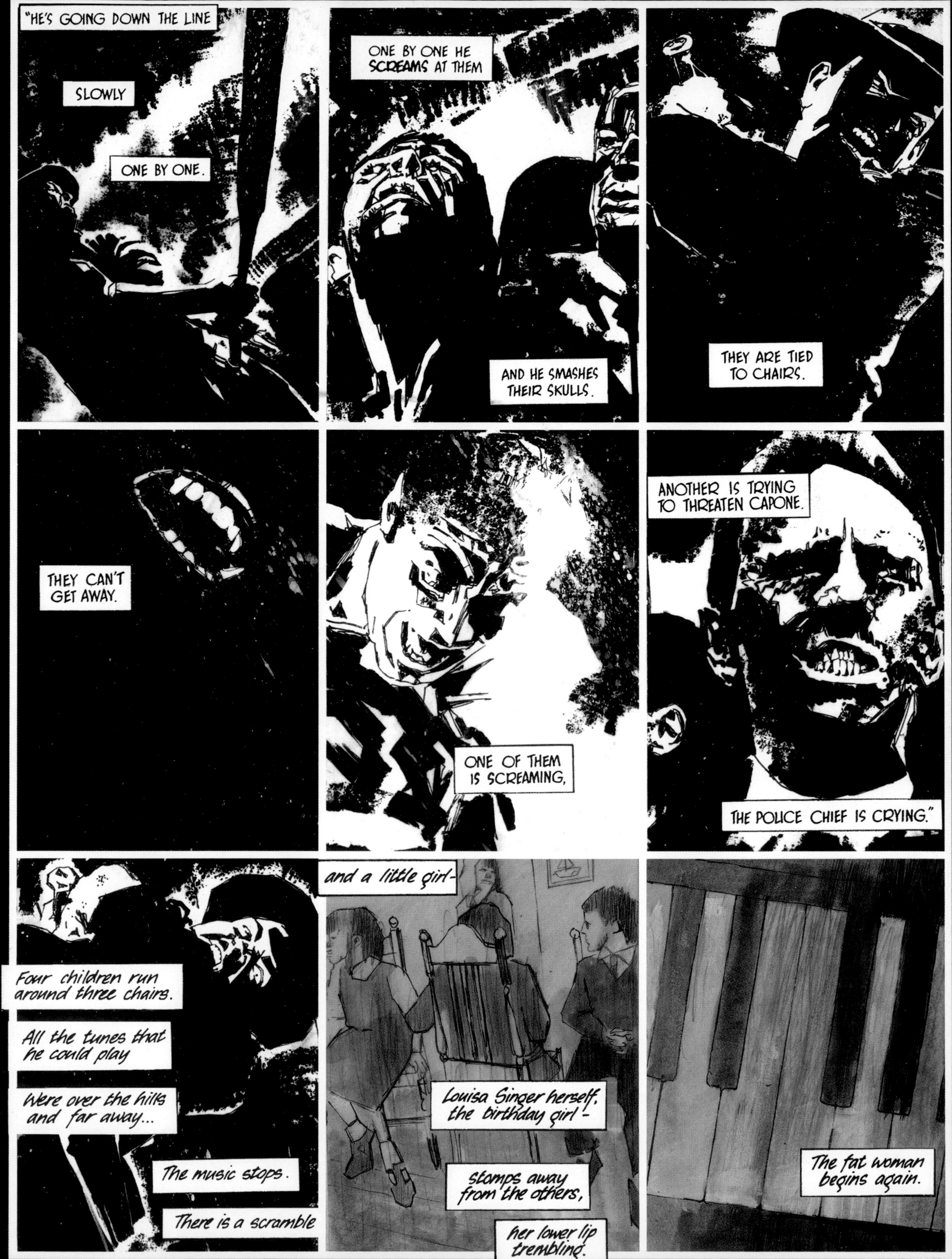

"HE'S GOING DOWN THE LINE
SLOWLY
ONE BY ONE.
ONE BY ONE HE SCREAMS AT THEM
AND HE SMASHES THEIR SKULLS.
THEY ARE TIED TO CHAIRS.
THEY CAN'T GET AWAY.
ONE OF THEM IS SCREAMING,
ANOTHER IS TRYING TO THREATEN CAPONE.
THE POLICE CHIEF IS CRYING."
Four children run around three chairs.
All the tunes that he could play
Were over the hills and far away...
The music stops.
There is a scramble
and a little girl-
Louisa Singer herself, the birthday girl -
stomps away from the others,
her lower lip trembling.
The fat woman begins again.

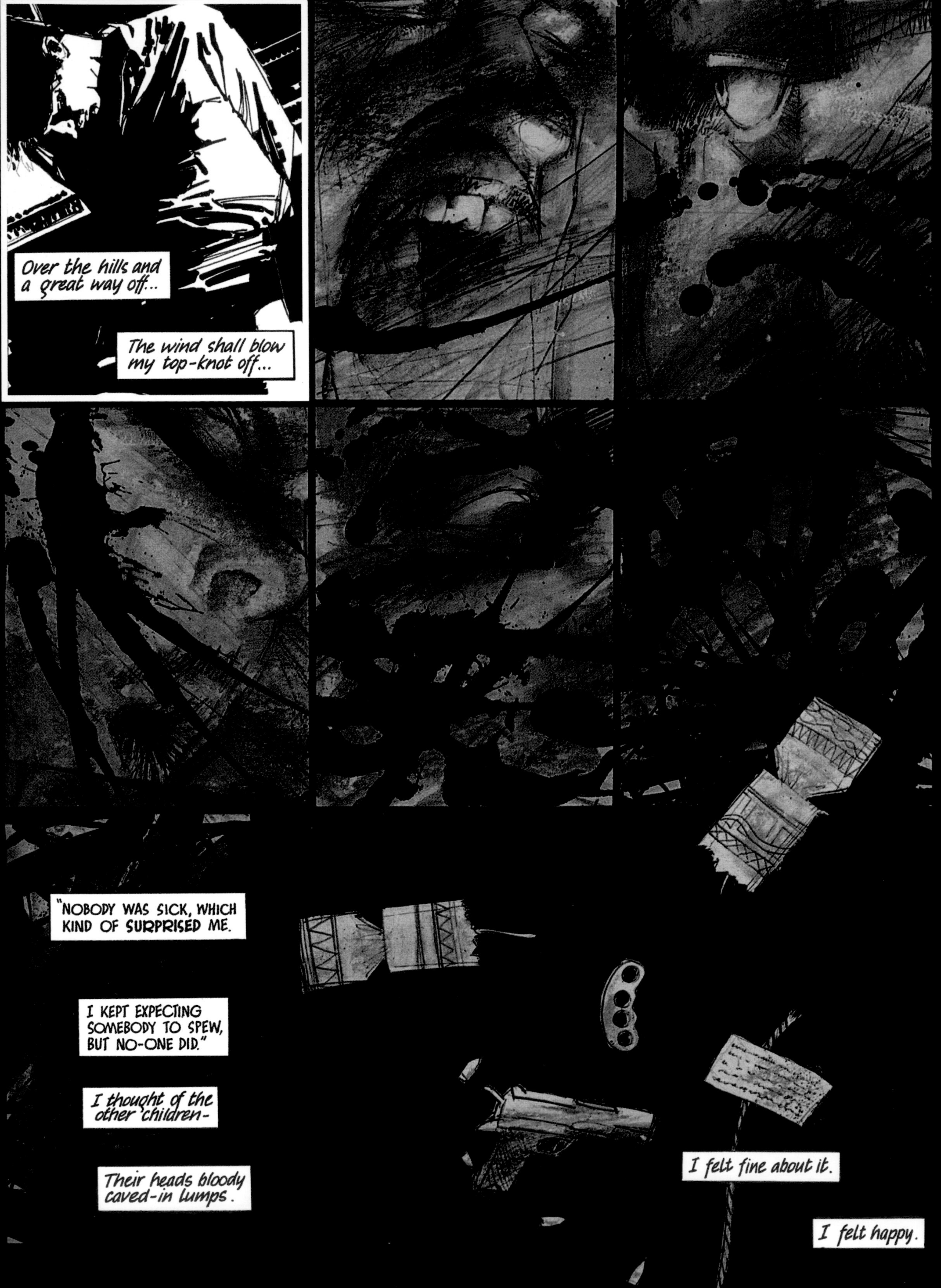
Over the hills and a great way off...
The wind shall blow my top-knot off...
"NOBODY WAS SICK, WHICH KIND OF SURPRISED ME.
I KEPT EXPECTING SOMEBODY TO SPEW, BUT NO-ONE DID."
I thought of the other children-
Their heads bloody caved-in lumps.
I felt fine about it.
I felt happy.

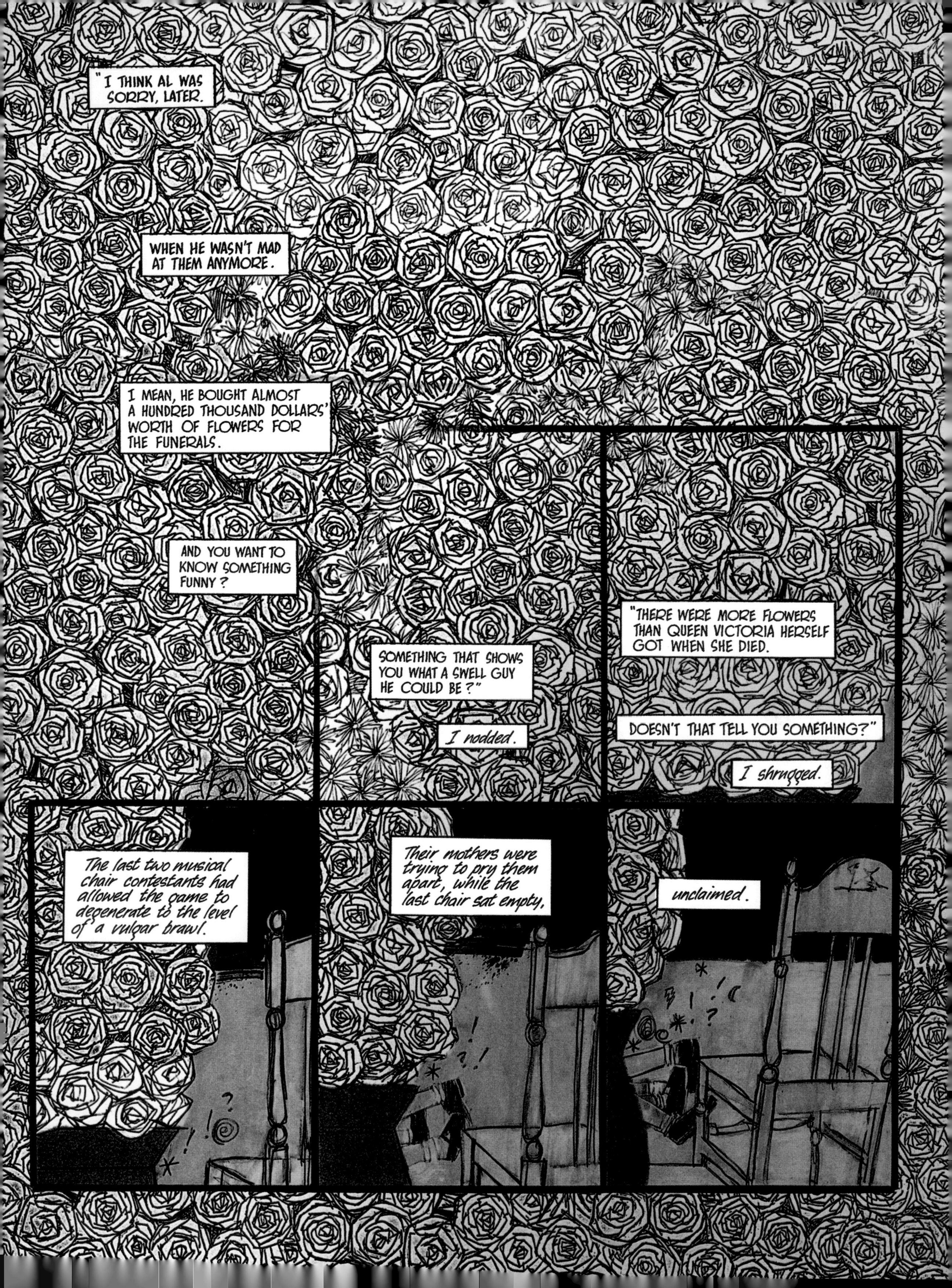
"I THINK AL WAS SORRY, LATER.
WHEN HE WASN'T MAD AT THEM ANYMORE.
I MEAN, HE BOUGHT ALMOST A HUNDRED THOUSAND DOLLARS' WORTH OF FLOWERS FOR THE FUNERALS.
AND YOU WANT TO KNOW SOMETHING FUNNY?
SOMETHING THAT SHOWS YOU WHAT A SWELL GUY HE COULD BE?"
I nodded.
"THERE WERE MORE FLOWERS THAN QUEEN VICTORIA HERSELF GOT WHEN SHE DIED.
DOESN'T THAT TELL YOU SOMETHING?"
I shrugged.
The last two musical chair contestants had allowed the game to degenerate to the level of a vulgar brawl.
Their mothers were trying to pry them apart, while the last chair sat empty,
unclaimed.

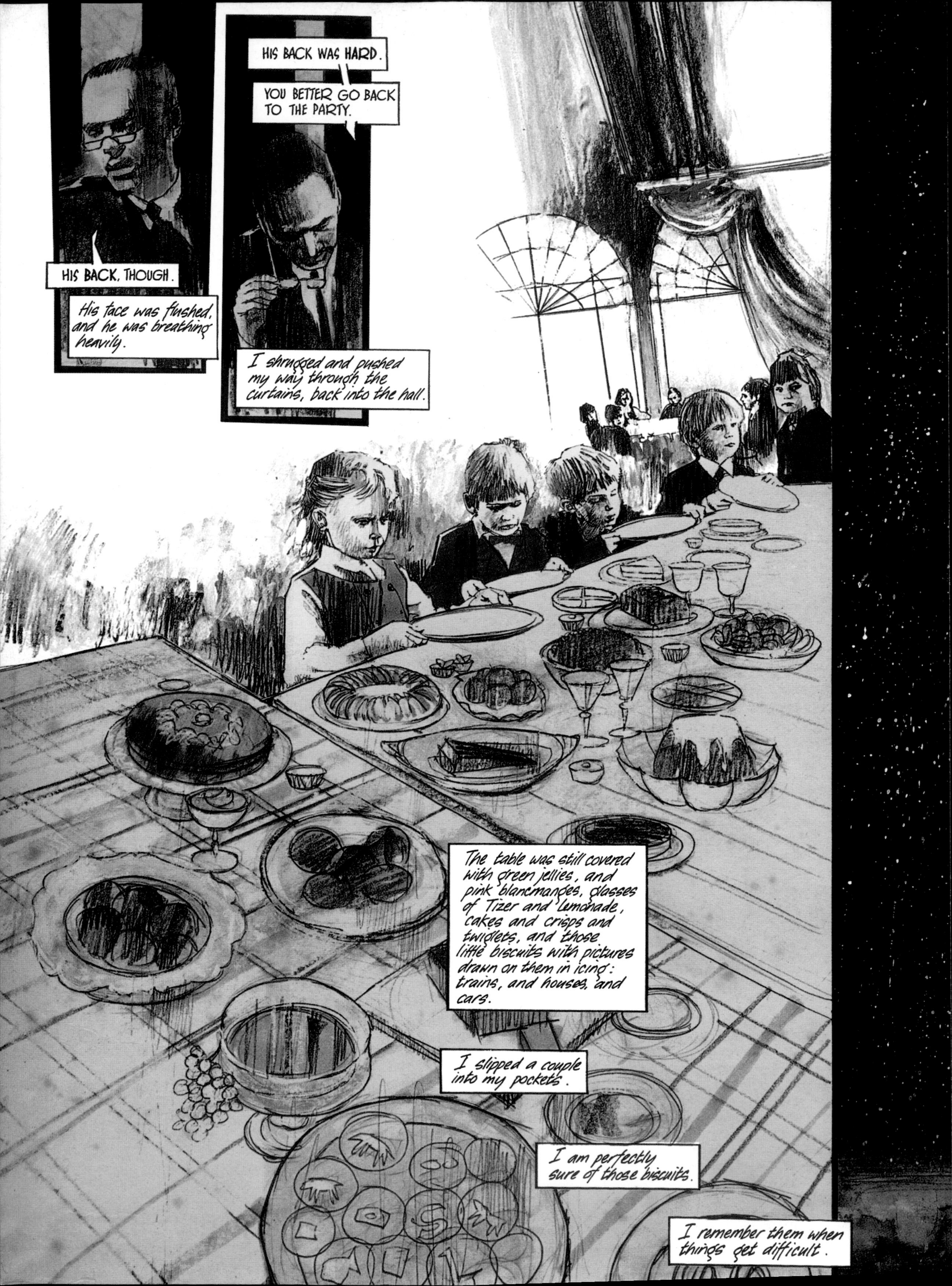
HIS BACK, THOUGH.
His face was flushed, and he was breathing heavily.
HIS BACK WAS HARD.
YOU BETTER GO BACK TO THE PARTY.
I shrugged and pushed my way through the curtains, back into the hall.
The table was still covered with green jellies, and pink blancmanges, glasses of Tizer and lemonade, cakes and crisps and twiglets, and those little biscuits with pictures drawn on them in icing: trains, and houses, and cars.
I slipped a couple into my pockets.
I am perfectly sure of those biscuits.
I remember them when things get difficult.

There are those bits of one's memory that simply do not work –

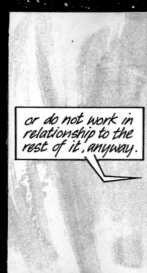

or do not work in relationship to the rest of it, anyway.

When I was sixteen I was walking home –

late at night under a sky hung with thousands of stars;

when my eye was caught by one star that seemed to be twinkling oddly.

The star became brighter as I looked at it, until it was the brightest thing in the sky –

although I should point out, it did not move–

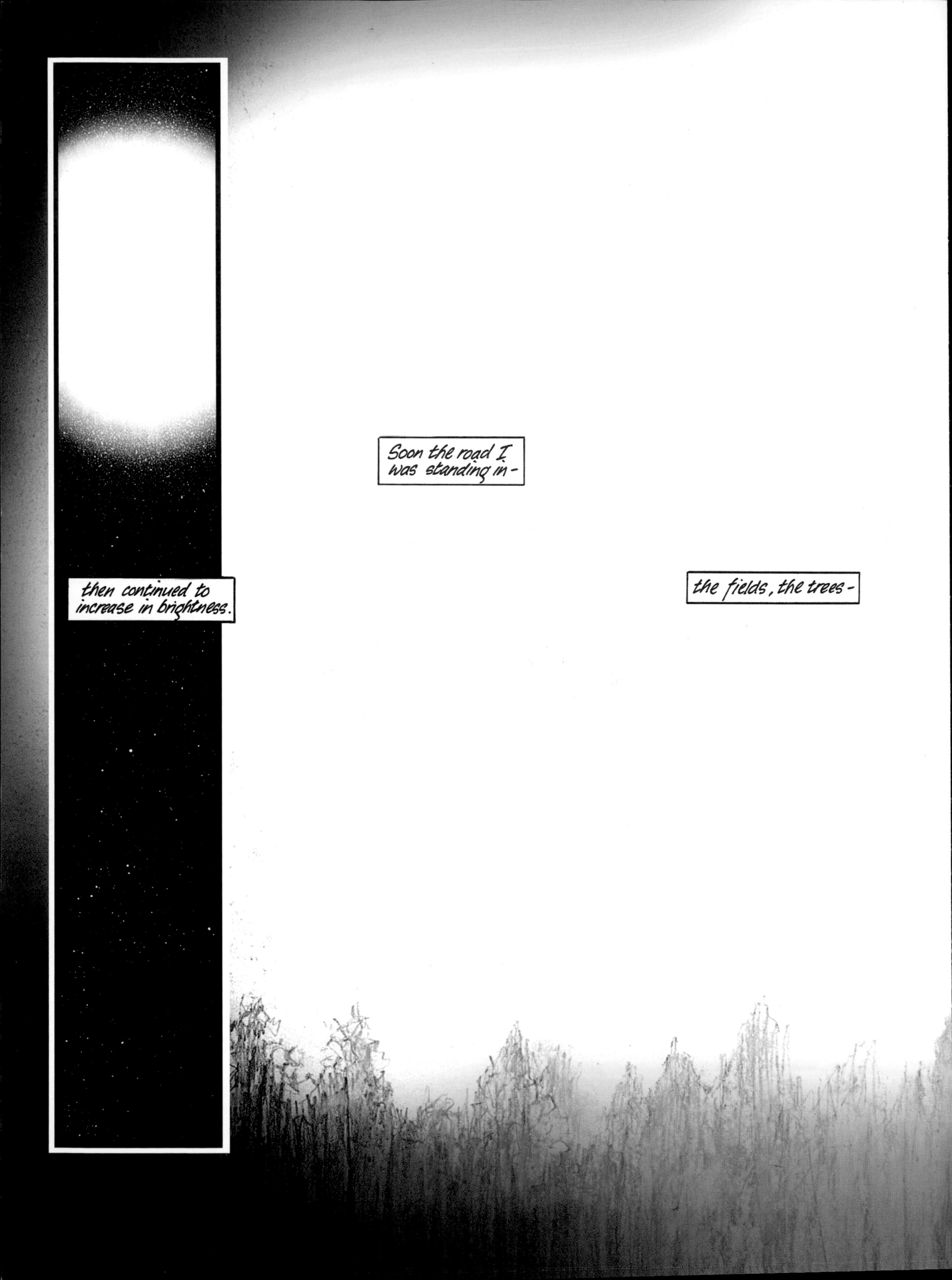
then continued to increase in brightness.
Soon the road I was standing in-
the fields, the trees-

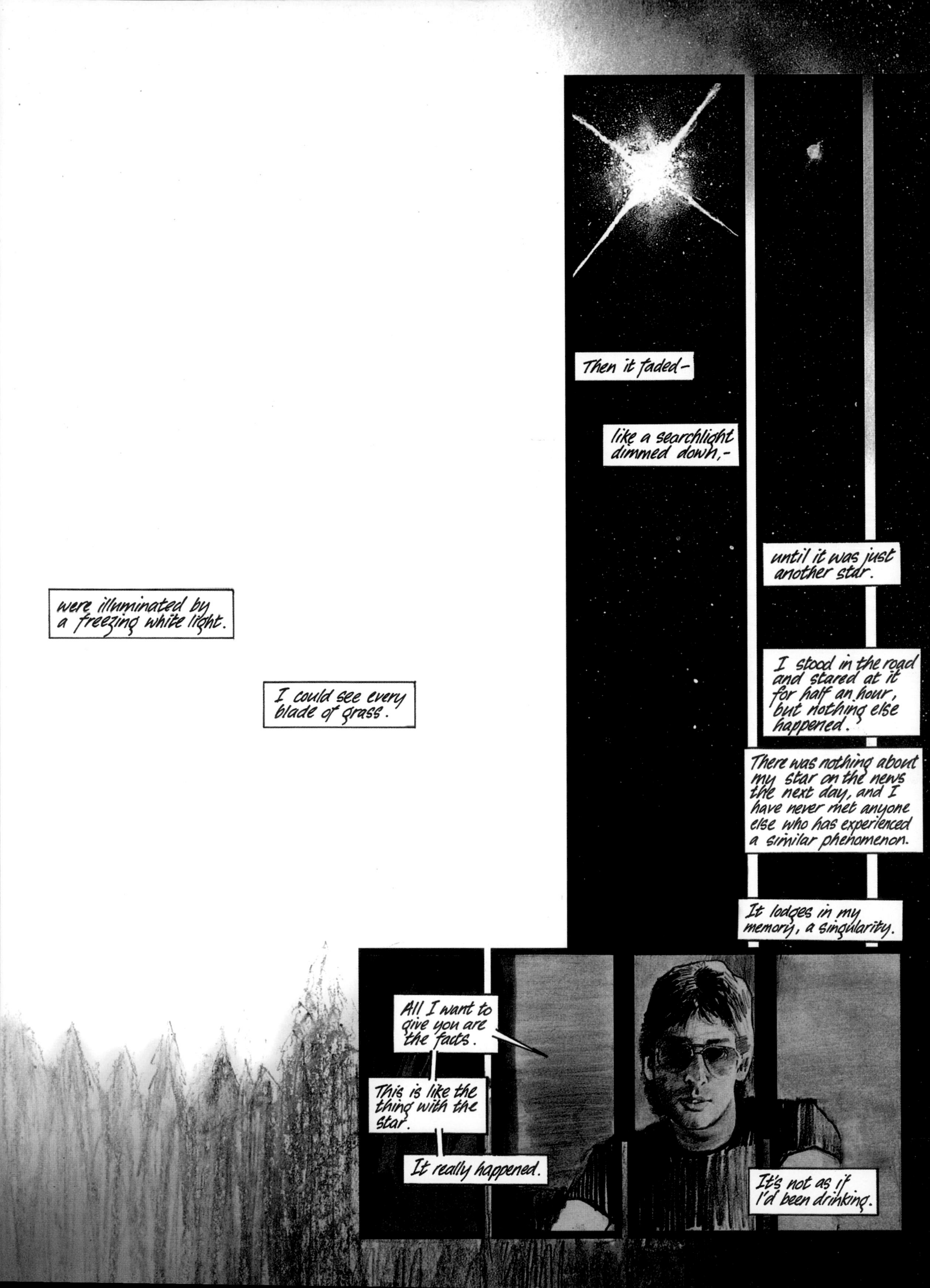
were illuminated by a freezing white light.
I could see every blade of grass.
Then it faded-
like a searchlight dimmed down,-
until it was just another star.
I stood in the road and stared at it for half an hour, but nothing else happened.
There was nothing about my star on the news the next day, and I have never met anyone else who has experienced a similar phenomenon.
It lodges in my memory, a singularity.
All I want to give you are the facts.
This is like the thing with the star.
It really happened.
It's not as if I'd been drinking.

The curtain in front of the bar began to shake.
I went back over to it, pulled it aside, peeked through.
Al Capone's osteopath was in conversation with the bald man.
He was crying.
The door opened and then three men came in -
three men in suits so elegant and strange that I could hardly keep from crying out -
until I saw the menace in their eyes.
They carried baseball bats.
The conjuror saw them first.
He pulled a cigar from his breast pocket, put it in his mouth, and lit it.
Then he sat back in his chair.
The osteopath finished his drink.
ALFRED HITCHCOCK'S
THE MAN WHO KNEW TOO MUCH
The three men wore hats.

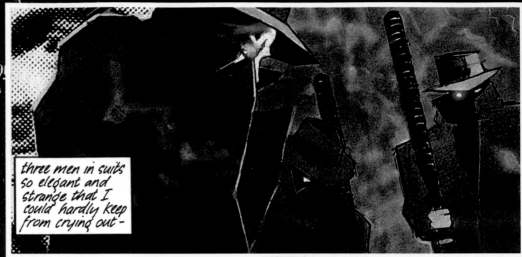

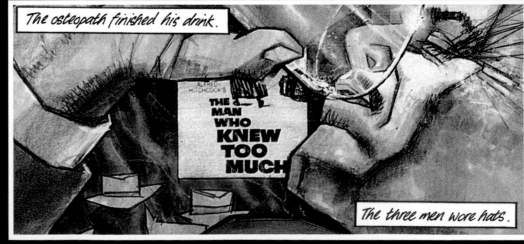

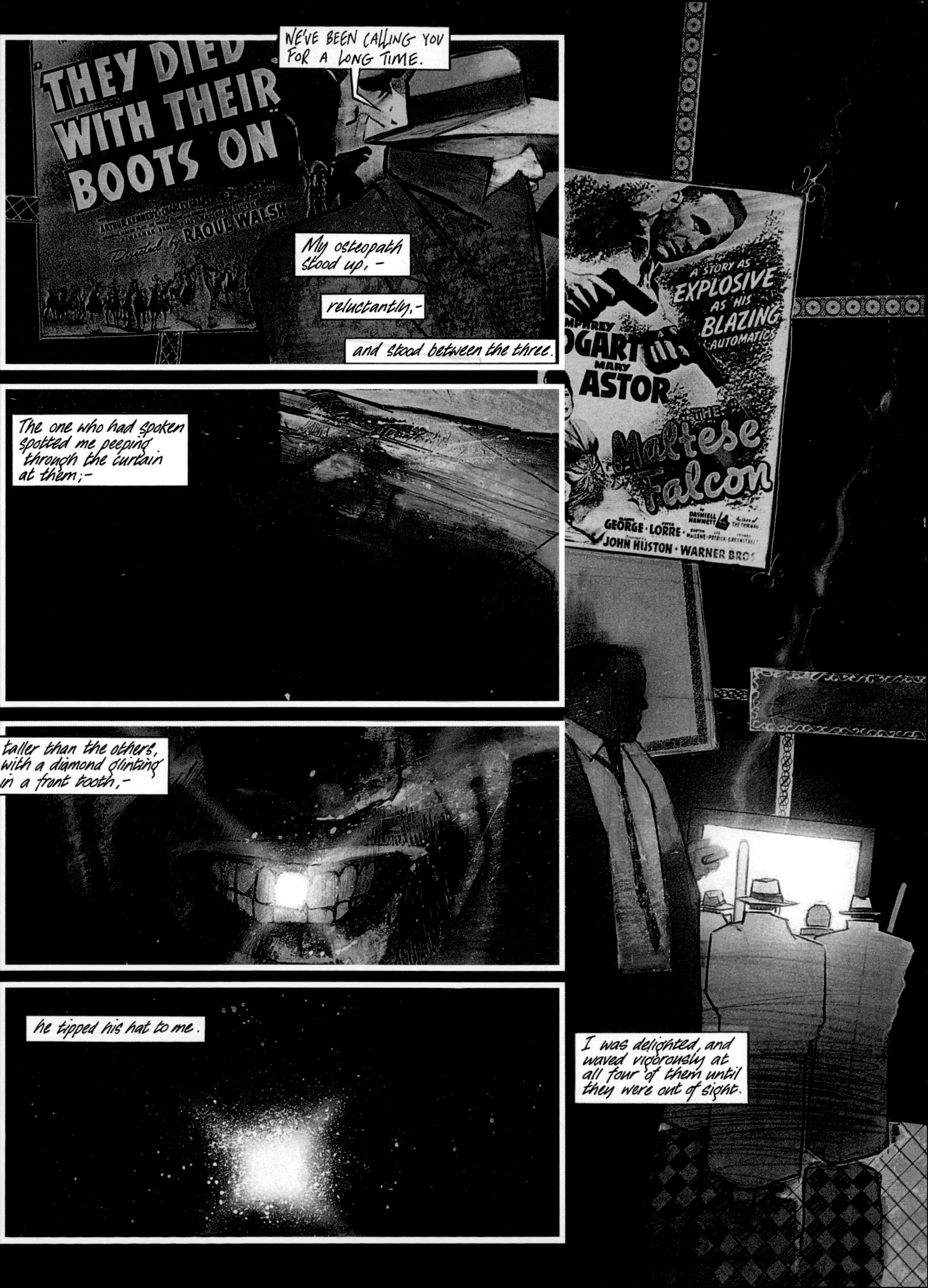

THEY DIED WITH THEIR BOOTS ON
RAOUL WALSH
WE'VE BEEN CALLING YOU FOR A LONG TIME.
My osteopath stood up, -
reluctantly,-
and stood between the three.
A STORY AS EXPLOSIVE AS HIS BLAZING AUTOMATICS
MARY ASTOR
The Maltese Falcon
GEORGE · LORRE
JOHN HUSTON · WARNER BROS
The one who had spoken spotted me peeping through the curtain at them;-
taller than the others, with a diamond glinting in a front tooth,-
he tipped his hat to me.
I was delighted, and waved vigorously at all four of them until they were out of sight.

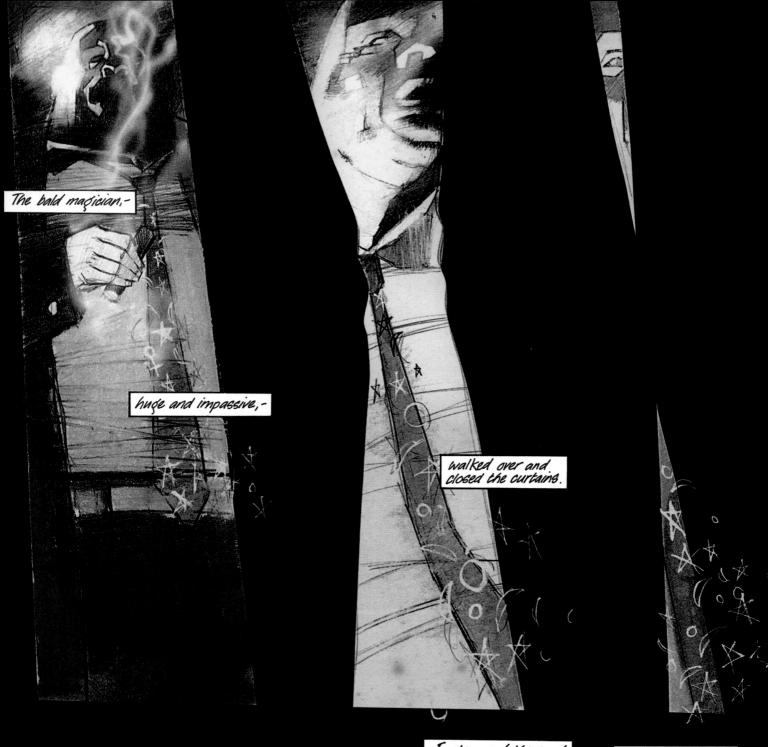

The bald magician,-

huge and impassive,-

walked over and closed the curtains.

I ate one of the sweet biscuits I had put into my pocket, crunching the icing between my teeth.

Then I went up to Louisa Singer and her mother, who were standing by the big door.

I said, "Thank you for having me."

Louisa's mother said, "You're welcome,"-

and I put on my coat with the velvet collar, and, accompanied by my parents, I made my way home.

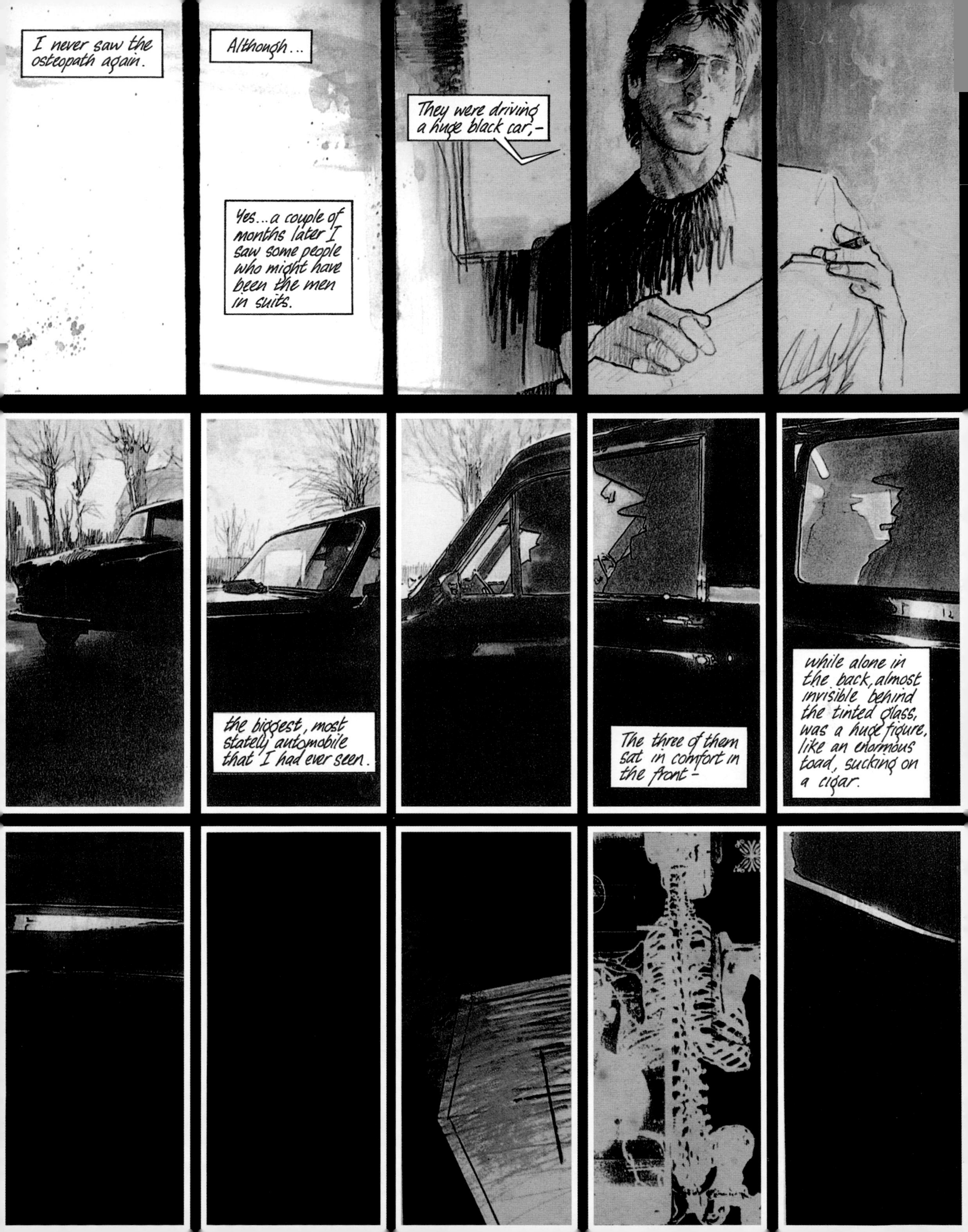
I never saw the osteopath again.
Although...
Yes... a couple of months later I saw some people who might have been the men in suits.
They were driving a huge black car, -
the biggest, most stately automobile that I had ever seen.
The three of them sat in comfort in the front -
while alone in the back, almost invisible behind the tinted glass, was a huge figure, like an enormous toad, sucking on a cigar.

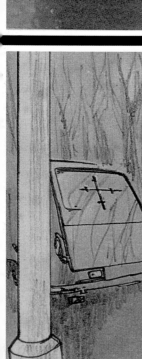

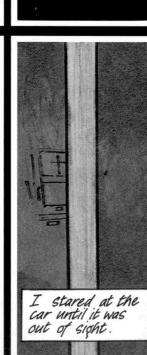

I stared at the car until it was out of sight.

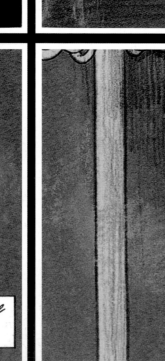

Nobody seems to wear a hat these days.

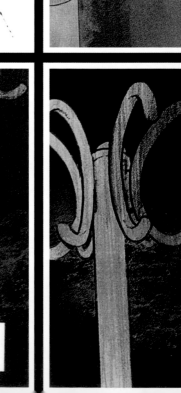

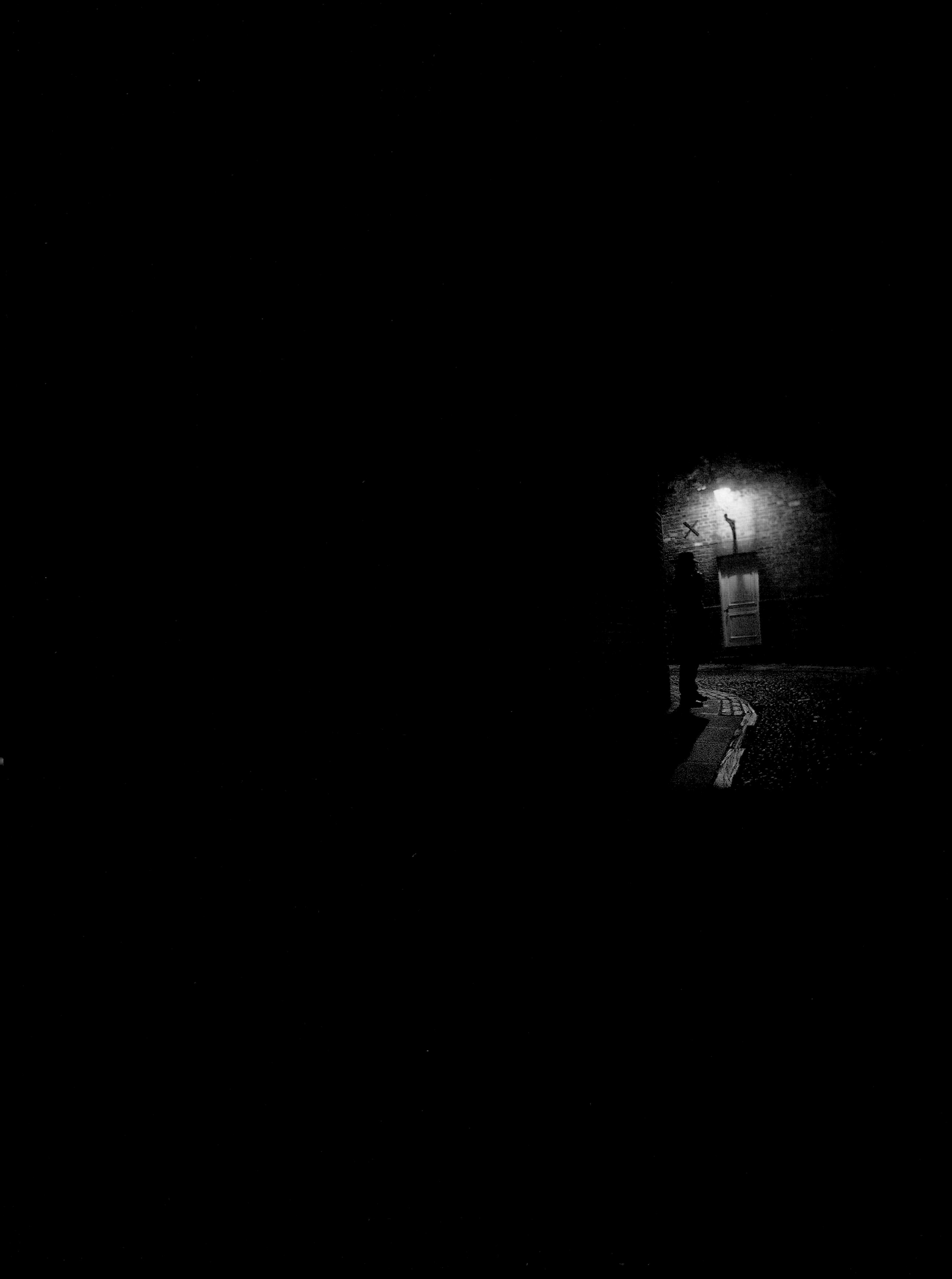

ALAN MOORE

For the past forty or fifty years, comic books have muddled through their infancy at a slow and sedentary pace. So slow, in fact, that it sometimes seemed as if it would last forever. Though the infant would frequently show signs of early promise, if not indeed genius, its physical progress never seemed to get beyond the crawling stage. This deceptive sluggishness often tended to mask the slow and occasionally painful process of maturation that the poor tyke was going through. Those of us in charge of minding the baby were so resigned to its eternal and unchanging state of mewling immaturity that even when the first bumps, swellings, sproutings, and secretions began to make their presence felt, we remained oblivious to what was actually going on. Then, one day, all of a sudden—Bang! It's puberty! Since then, comics have been changing so fast that we scarcely recognize the snub-nosed toddler that we used to call "Freckles." In its place there's something spotty and gawky and strange looking, that's asking a lot of awkward questions about sex and politics, while striking unfamiliar attitudes and dressing itself in colours nobody over twenty-five would be seen dead in. Its utterances range from the unbearably crass to the undeniably brilliant, and though its self-consciousness may prove irritating every now and then, it's still possible to catch glimpses of the confident and fascinating adult persona that it's struggling towards.

Suddenly caught up in the turbulent adolescence of an art form, those of us currently working in the medium find events happening too fast for us to make coherent sense of. That the critics, public, and creators themselves are taking comics more seriously seems undeniable. Comics are starting to be viewed as a vibrant and viable art form, rich in unexplored possibilities and hidden capacities. As a result, new talents that might otherwise easily have drifted into films or fine art or literature are starting to find their way to the medium and enriching it considerably by their presence. As this process gathers momentum, comics find themselves on the verge of a quantum leap in which all the old barriers are shattered and the territory becomes strange and different, entirely without landmark.

Thanks to the new audience that exists for work of interesting content and high quality, creators need no longer shackle themselves to the demands of the superhero market. They can explore new concepts, new styles and approaches, secure in the knowledge that a body of readership exists which will support them. The fruits of this fortunate situation are just beginning to appear, and I'm happy to report that it looks like a good harvest—at least if the volume in your hands is anything to go by.

Violent Cases started life as a short story crafted by author Neil Gaiman for the Milford science fiction writers' workshop. Though powerful and affecting in its blend of reality, remembrance, and fantasy, it might well have ended life there, were it not for the happy and unexpected conjunction of Gaiman's undoubted talents with those of the remarkable Dave McKean.

McKean, to make the obvious comparison and get it out of the way, has been inspired in the basic eclectic nature of his work by that of Bill Sienkiewicz. That said, I hope no one will let such a glib comparison blind them to the fact that everything else in McKean's work is pure Dave McKean—and by that I mean the imagination, the mastery of graphic effect, the sheer artistry of this extraordinary material. It seems almost embarrassingly obvious to suggest that this sickeningly young artist is going to be enormous in his impact on the field, rather like suggesting that the bombing of Hiroshima was likely to be quite noisy.

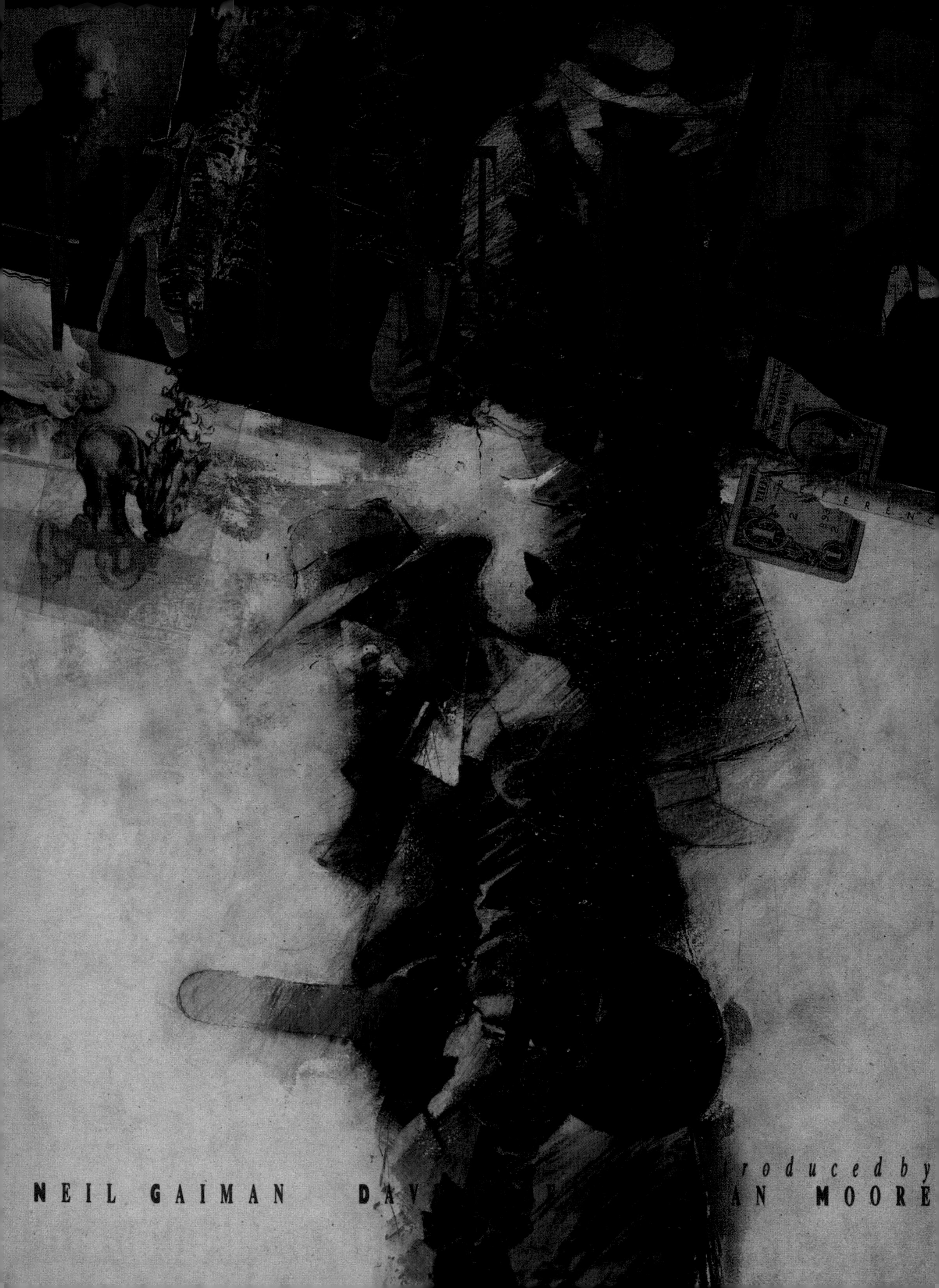
roducedby
NEIL GAIMAN
DAV
AN MOORE

Quite aside from his own talent, McKean is doubly blessed by his collaboration with Neil Gaiman. Though originating outside the comic book field, Gaiman is a writer of some years' experience who blends a confident and lucid sense of narrative with a sensibility every bit as eclectic as that found in his partner's visual representations. Here we have a writer aware of what is happening in the broader fields of literature beyond the confines of the comics world, bringing that knowledge to bear upon this new art form and in the process managing to create a quietly ambitious piece of work that, in its own way, begins to chart some of the new areas of potential that lie in the medium's future.

Violent Cases isn't a novel; it started life as a short story and in terms of word length still does not go beyond that classification. In its effect, however, it clearly accomplishes something quite different. The texture and subtleties of meaning that the prose and artwork bring forth from their conjunction make this a work of rich complexity that rewards repeated examination and elicits responses that a short story in its unillustrated form would clearly be incapable of. This is something new. Its stylistic nuances defy classification as easily as does its genre. Part childhood memory, part reconstruction of a violent past, part comment upon the magic to be gleaned from remembered events, *Violent Cases* evokes unfamiliar feelings in an unfamiliar way. In doing so it promises much for the future output of its creators, whether singly or together, and promises more for the future of the medium as a whole.

With these strong and confident steps towards that medium's maturity, it becomes very clear that events will no longer be proceeding at a crawl. Next thing you know, the kid will be learning to drive, and won't that be something?

Alan Moore
Northampton, 1987

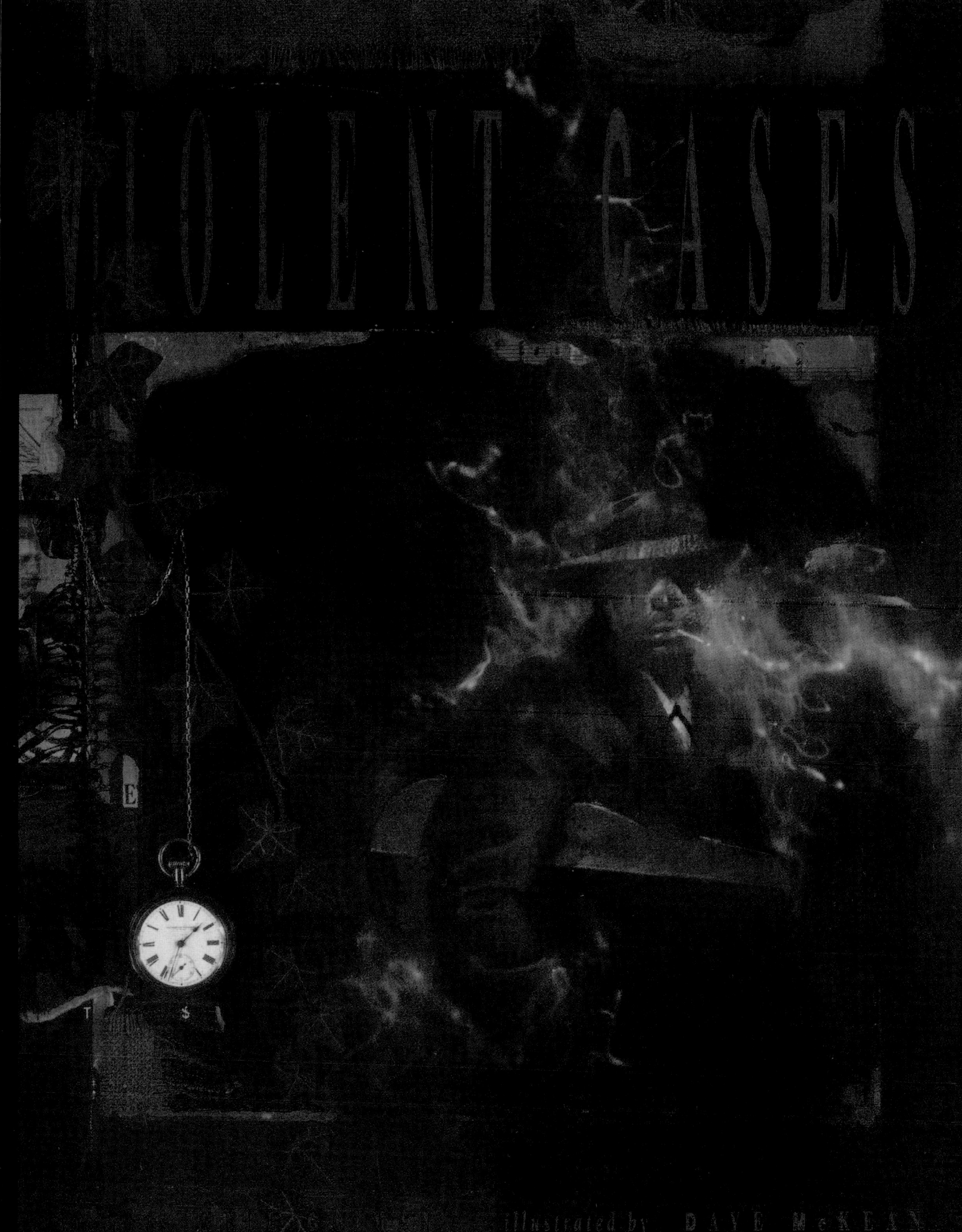
VIOLENT CASES
illustrated by DAVE McKEAN

INTRODUCTION
From the 1991 reissue of Violent Cases
Neil Gaiman

In 1986, I met Dave McKean.

He was still at art college. I was a young journalist. Both of us had been recruited to work for a Bright New British Anthology Comic (the title doesn't matter—it never came out, and I doubt the world has lost anything by its absence). He was drawing two strips; I was writing three other strips. Both of us had very definite ideas about the kind of comics we wanted to see, the kind of comics we liked.

They were heady times. We were both intoxicated by the potential of the medium, by the then-strange idea that comics weren't exclusively for kids anymore (if they had ever been): that the possibilities were endless.

Dave went to New York for a week and showed his portfolio to all the comics publishers he could find. They stared at him blankly and sent him home. I wrote articles for British magazines and newspapers, doing my best to tell the world about *Maus, Watchmen, Love & Rockets, Elektra: Assassin.* The Good Stuff that was out there.

In England, much of the brightest work was being showcased in *Escape,* a magazine edited by Paul Gravett. He did an article on the Bright New Anthology Comic Dave and I were working for, and liked my writing, liked Dave's art, asked if we'd be willing to work together and contribute a five-page strip to *Escape.* We agreed enthusiastically.

We talked about what we wanted to do: a comic for people who didn't read comics; something with no superheroes, no science fiction, no overt genre elements; something we could show our friends, and that our friends would read, and, if we were lucky, respect.

I went away and thought.

One of the things that had impressed me most about the work of Dave's I'd seen so far, leaving aside his simple ability to draw the pants off most of his contemporaries, was his sense of storytelling and design. I knew that if I was going to write something for him to draw, I was going to let him tell the story, let him discover the panel progressions.

Very well. I would write the words; Dave would draw the pictures.

I finished the story—skein of words with picture-sized gaps in the text—but I didn't have a title for it. I took the story to the Milford writers' workshop, and was told it was good, and Garry Kilworth pointed out the title to me: it was sitting in the text, wasn't it? I gave the manuscript to Dave, and he was keen to start. We went to see Paul Gravett, and explained a little hesitantly that what we were looking at doing was a forty-four-page graphic novel. Would he still be willing to publish it? He was. Dave did layouts, we argued about them; he requested changes in the text, we argued about them; it was great. He started to paint.

Somewhere in all that, the Bright New British Anthology Comic snuffled in pain, rolled over, and died. We hardly noticed—we were off in a world of old photographs and snippets of cloth and ivy leaves, of gangsters and osteopaths and childhood parties.

At last! Available in splendid glorious original full color!

NEIL GAIMAN & DAVE McKEAN'S

VIOLENT

We finished it in early 1987. Alan Moore wrote an introduction, and various good people gave us quotes for the back cover. And in late 1987, it was published in the UK by Titan Books, in association with *Escape*. In black and white.

NOW LET'S FAST-FORWARD A FEW YEARS (skipping over the things that happened to Dave, myself, and *Violent Cases* in the meantime, which, in the case of the latter, include being in print continuously since it came out, being adapted into a stage play, and astonishing both of us by winning more than its fair share of awards) to the arrival of Tundra. They expressed an interest in publishing an American edition of *Violent Cases*. Both Dave and I were excited: it had never been properly distributed in America, and only those few people who had been fortunate enough to look at Dave's original art had ever seen the wonderful chromatic range of blues and greys and browns he had introduced. This was *Violent Cases* as it was always meant to be.

And while both Dave and I have done many things since this book, together and apart, sometimes with less success, sometimes, I hope, with more, this is where it all started; this was where we began.

And while one's feelings for one's children (and, by the same token, for one's parents) must always be mixed, and while it is unwise to show favoritism, *Violent Cases* was our first child, and it commands from both of us a love and loyalty that's all its own. We're still proud of it. Especially now, dressed for a party, in its fine new colored coat.

Neil Gaiman
Sussex, March 1991

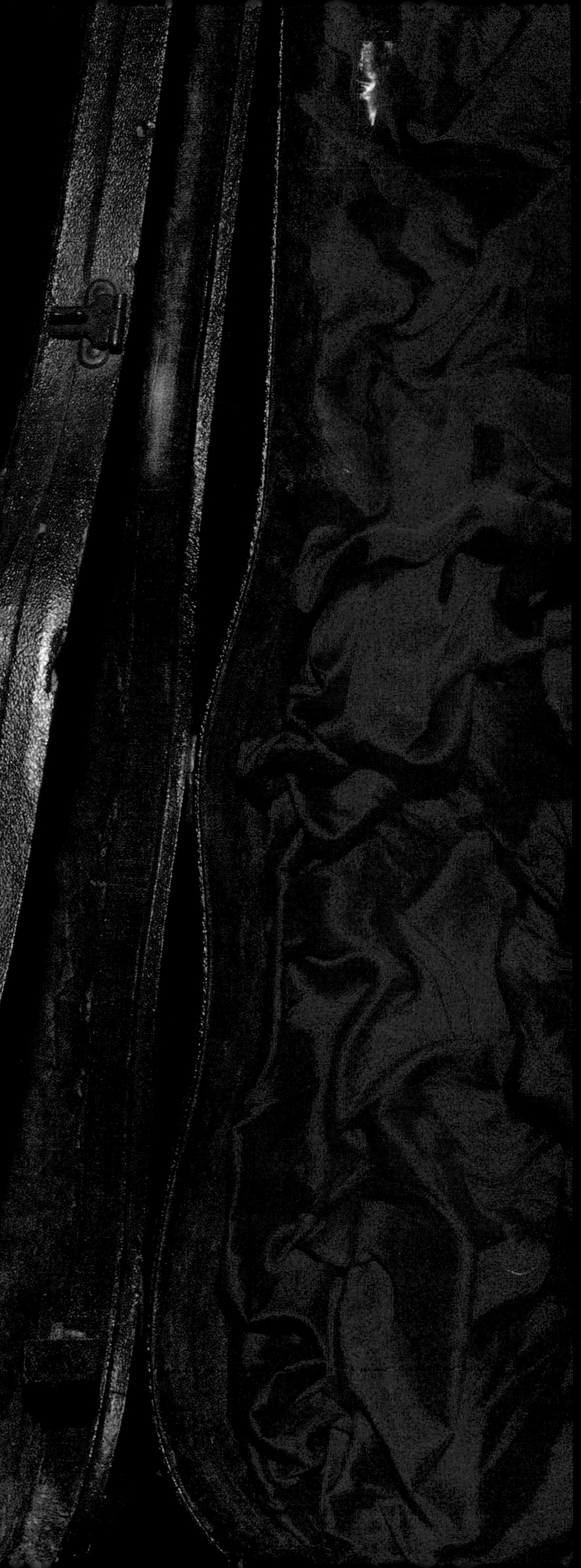

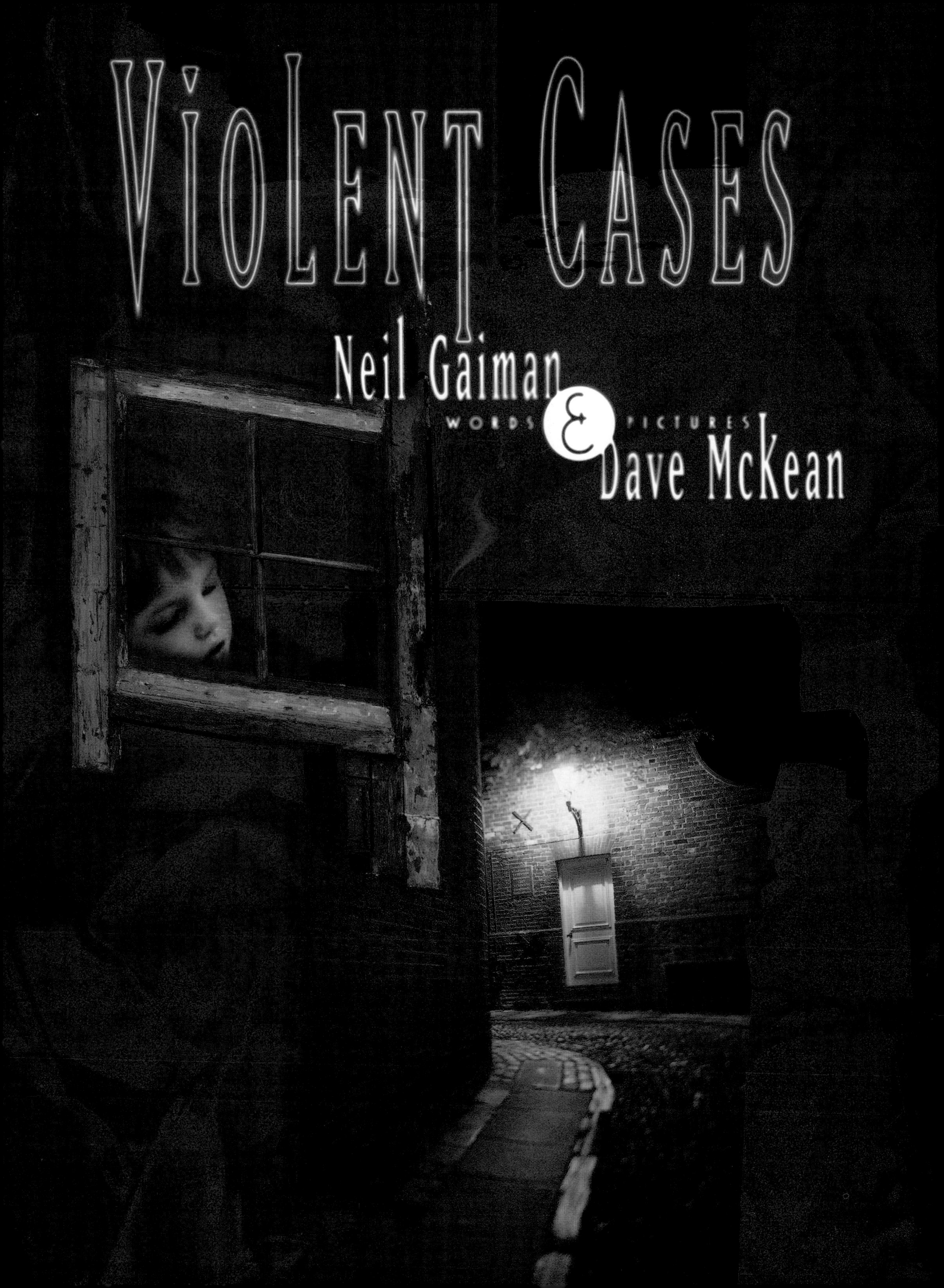
VIOLENT CASES
Neil Gaiman
WORDS
&
PICTURES
Dave McKean

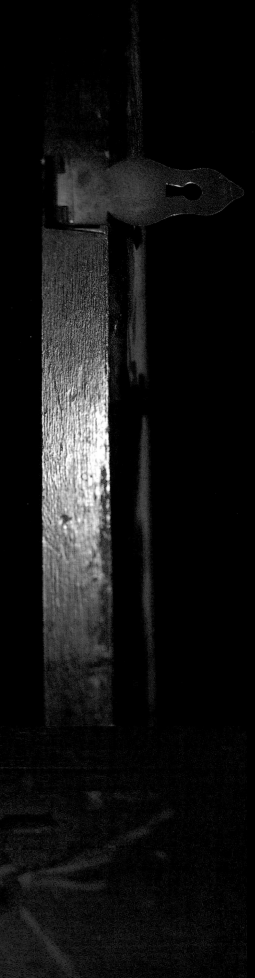

AFTERWORD
From the 2003 reissue of Violent Cases

I spent today with Dave McKean, more or less. He was in a huge blue studio, directing our first feature film, *MirrorMask*, while I walked a journalist around, and did the interviews that he was too busy to do (my part, the writing, being mostly over, after all). At one point the journalist asked how we started out, and we told him about *Violent Cases*, seventeen years ago. My daughter, Holly, who was eighteen a few days ago, asked Dave, "When did you first meet me?" and Dave thought for a moment, and said, "When I came over to your flat to take photos of Mike for *Violent Cases*. You weren't walking yet."

It's a book about time and memory, and the time has passed, and enough time that memory plays tricks on us, and the young man who lights his cigarette in the opening panels is not the middle-aged me who gave up smoking a decade ago. But he and Dave did something very fine a long time ago, and I'm still proud of them.

Neil Gaiman
July 2003

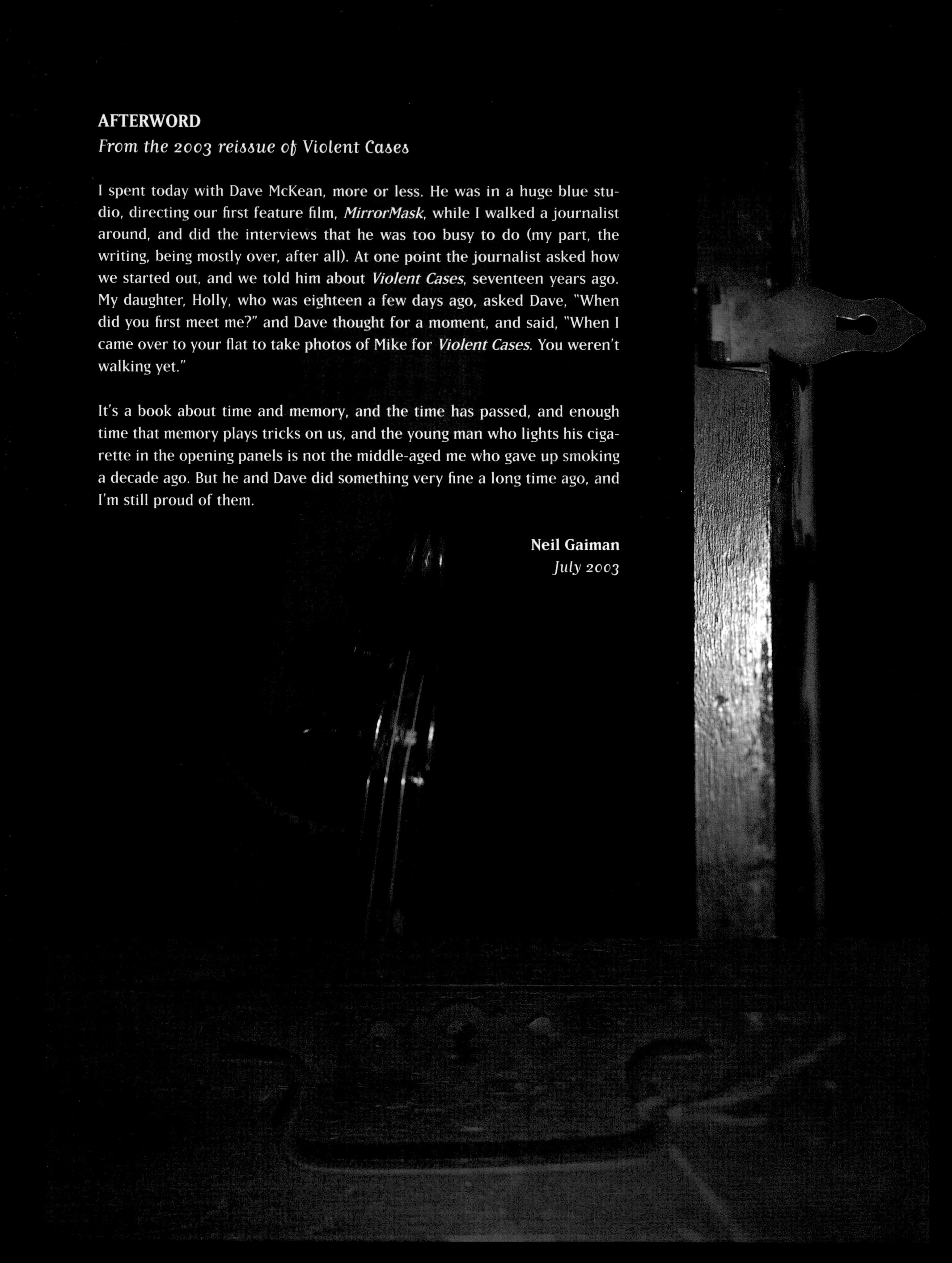

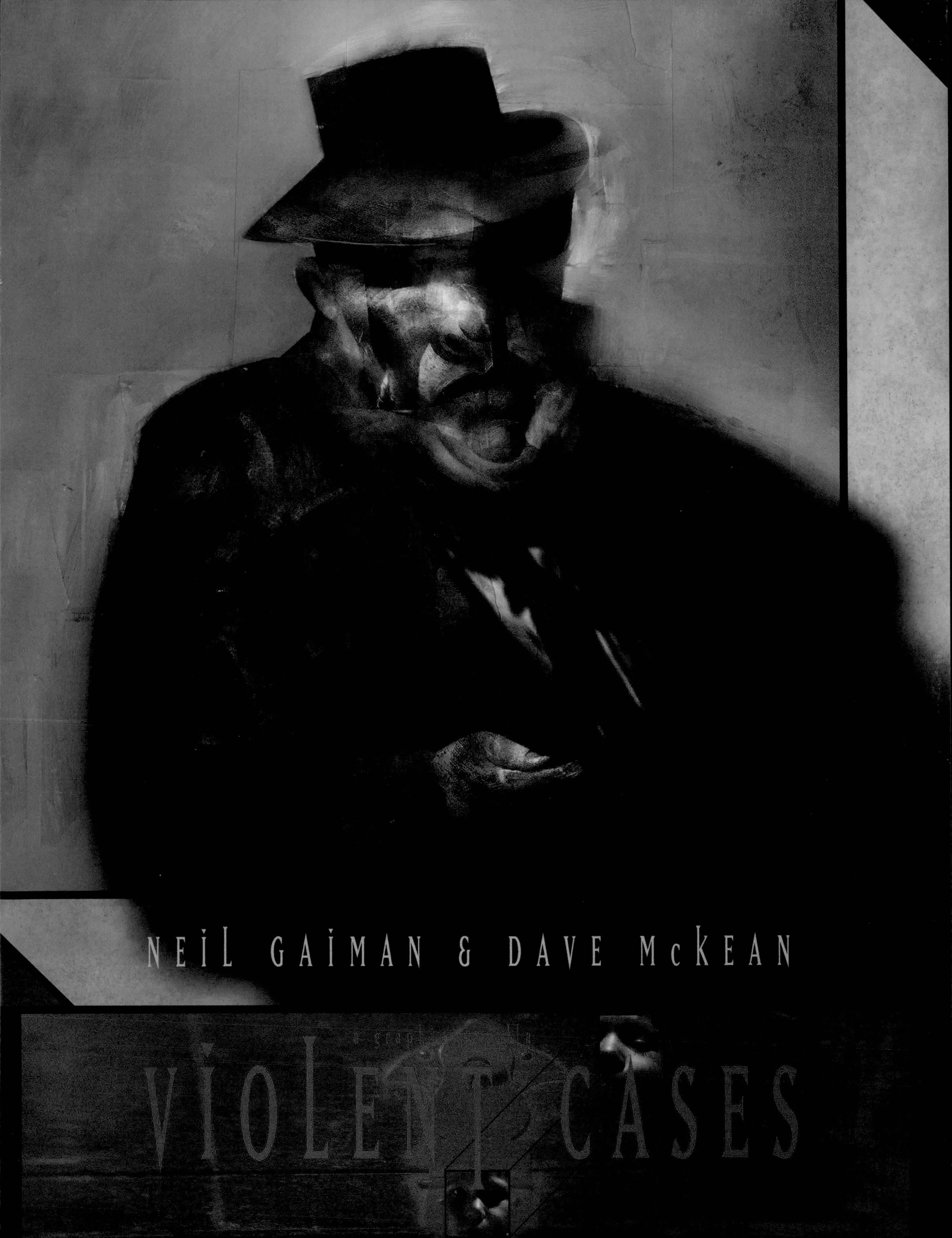
NEIL GAIMAN & DAVE McKEAN
VIOLENT CASES

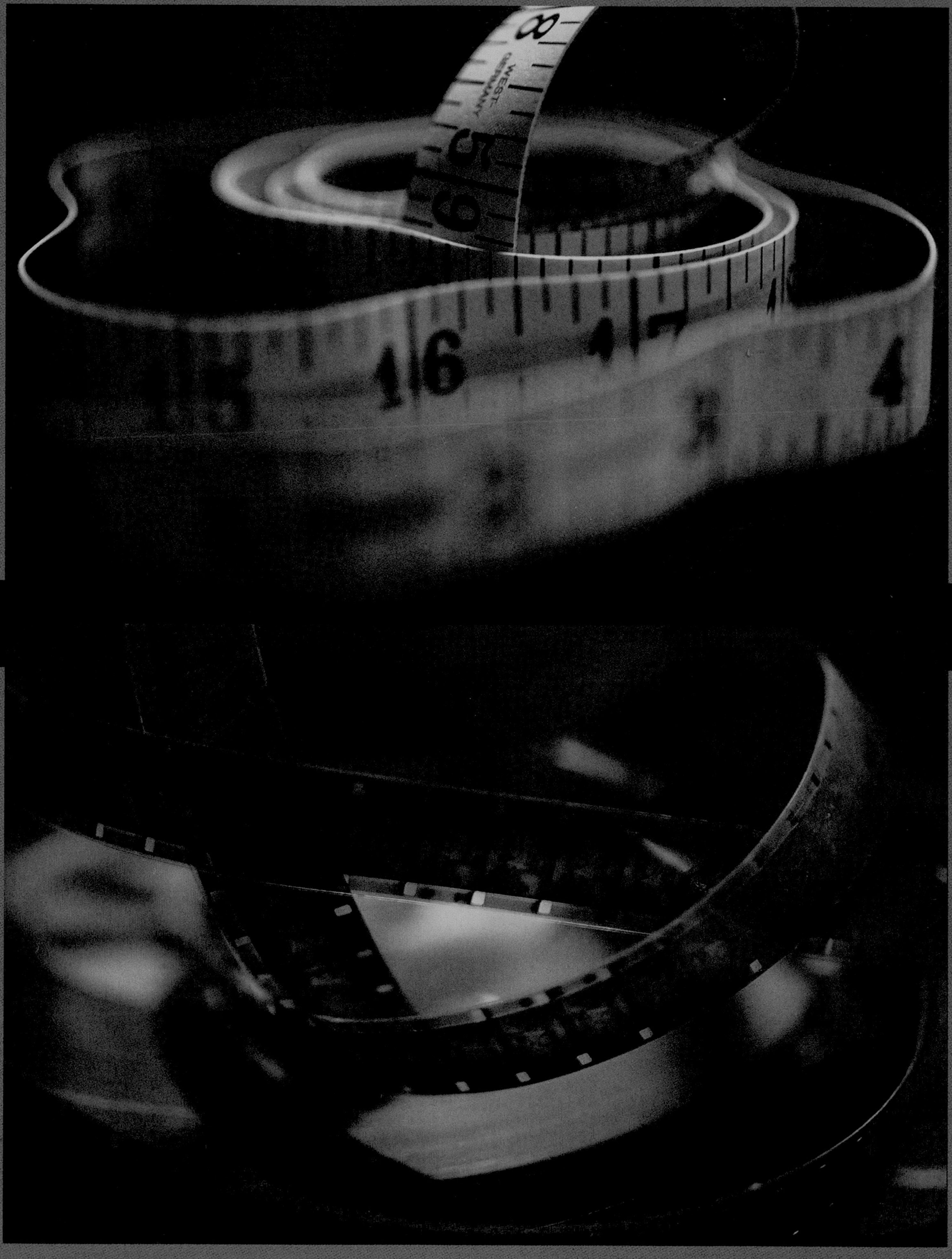
16

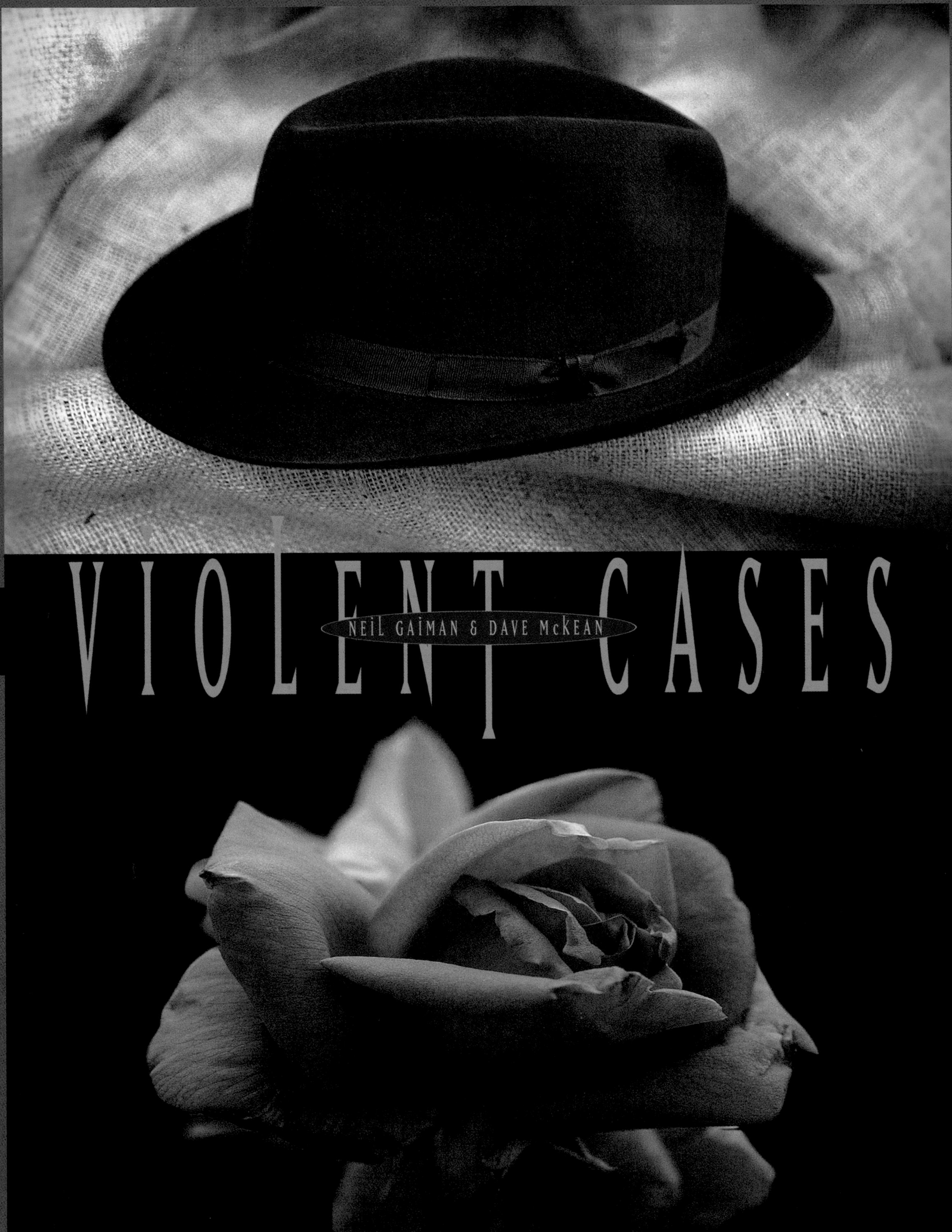
VIOLENT CASES
NEIL GAIMAN & DAVE McKEAN

BIOGRAPHIES

Neil Gaiman is the *New York Times* best-selling author of the novels ***Neverwhere, Stardust, American Gods, Anansi Boys*** (number-one *NYT* bestseller), and ***Good Omens*** (with **Terry Pratchett**); the ***Sandman*** series of graphic novels; and the short story collections ***Smoke and Mirrors*** and ***Fragile Things***. He is also the author of books for readers of all ages, including the number-one best-selling and Newbery Medal–winning novel ***The Graveyard Book***, the best-selling novels ***Coraline*** and ***Odd and the Frost Giants***; the short story collection ***M Is for Magic***, and the picture books ***The Wolves in the Walls, The Day I Swapped My Dad for Two Goldfish***, and ***Crazy Hair***, illustrated by **Dave McKean**; ***The Dangerous Alphabet***, illustrated by **Gris Grimly**; and ***Blueberry Girl***, illustrated by **Charles Vess**. He is the winner of numerous literary honors, including the Hugo, Bram Stoker, and World Fantasy Awards, and the Newbery Medal. Originally from England, he now lives in America. Visit him online at *neilgaiman.com*.

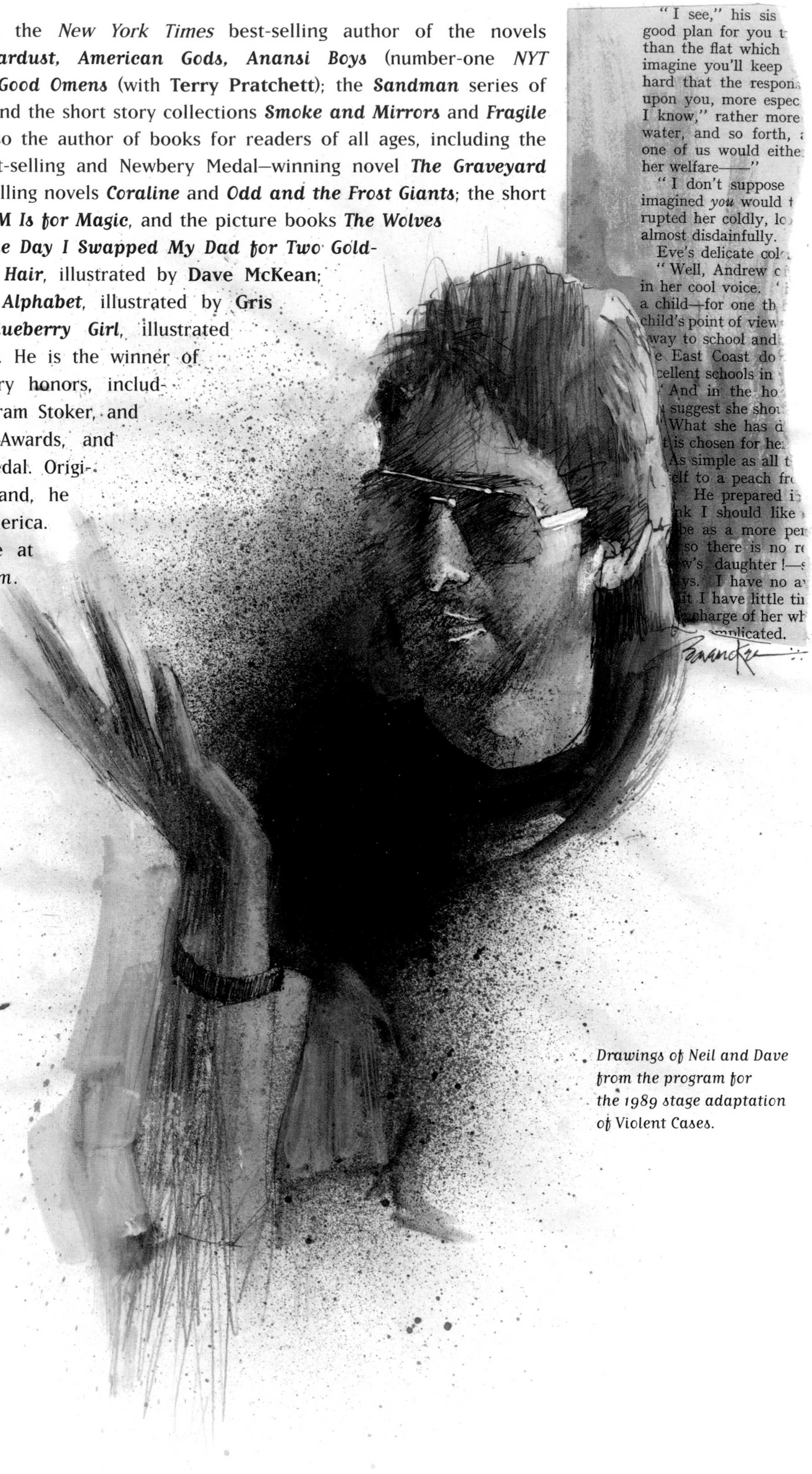

"I see," his sis
good plan for you
than the flat which
imagine you'll keep
hard that the respon
upon you, more espec
I know," rather more
water, and so forth,
one of us would eithe
her welfare——"
"I don't suppose
imagined *you* would
rupted her coldly, lo
almost disdainfully.
Eve's delicate col
"Well, Andrew
in her cool voice.
a child—for one th
child's point of view
way to school and
East Coast do
cellent schools in
And in the ho
suggest she shou
What she has d
is chosen for he
As simple as all
elf to a peach fr
He prepared i
nk I should like
be as a more pe
so there is no r
w's daughter !—
ys. I have no a
t I have little ti
harge of her wh
mplicated.

Drawings of Neil and Dave from the program for the 1989 stage adaptation of Violent Cases.

Dave McKean has illustrated and designed many award-winning and groundbreaking books and graphic novels, including ***The Magic of Reality*** **(Richard Dawkins)**, ***The Homecoming*** (Ray Bradbury), ***Varjak Paw*** (SF Said), ***The Savage, Slog's Dad***, and ***Mouse Bird Snake Wolf*** **(David Almond)**, ***The Fat Duck Cookbook*** and ***Historical Heston*** **(Heston Blumenthal)**, ***What's Welsh for Zen*** **(John Cale)**, ***Arkham Asylum*** **(Grant Morrison)**, ***Wizard & Glass*** **(Stephen King)**, and ***Mr. Punch, Signal to Noise, Coraline***, and the Newbery and Carnegie Medal winning ***The Graveyard Book*** **(Neil Gaiman)**. His self-penned ***Cages*** received several awards for best graphic novel. He has also written and illustrated ***Pictures That Tick*** (a collection of short comics) and ***Celluloid*** (an erotic novel).

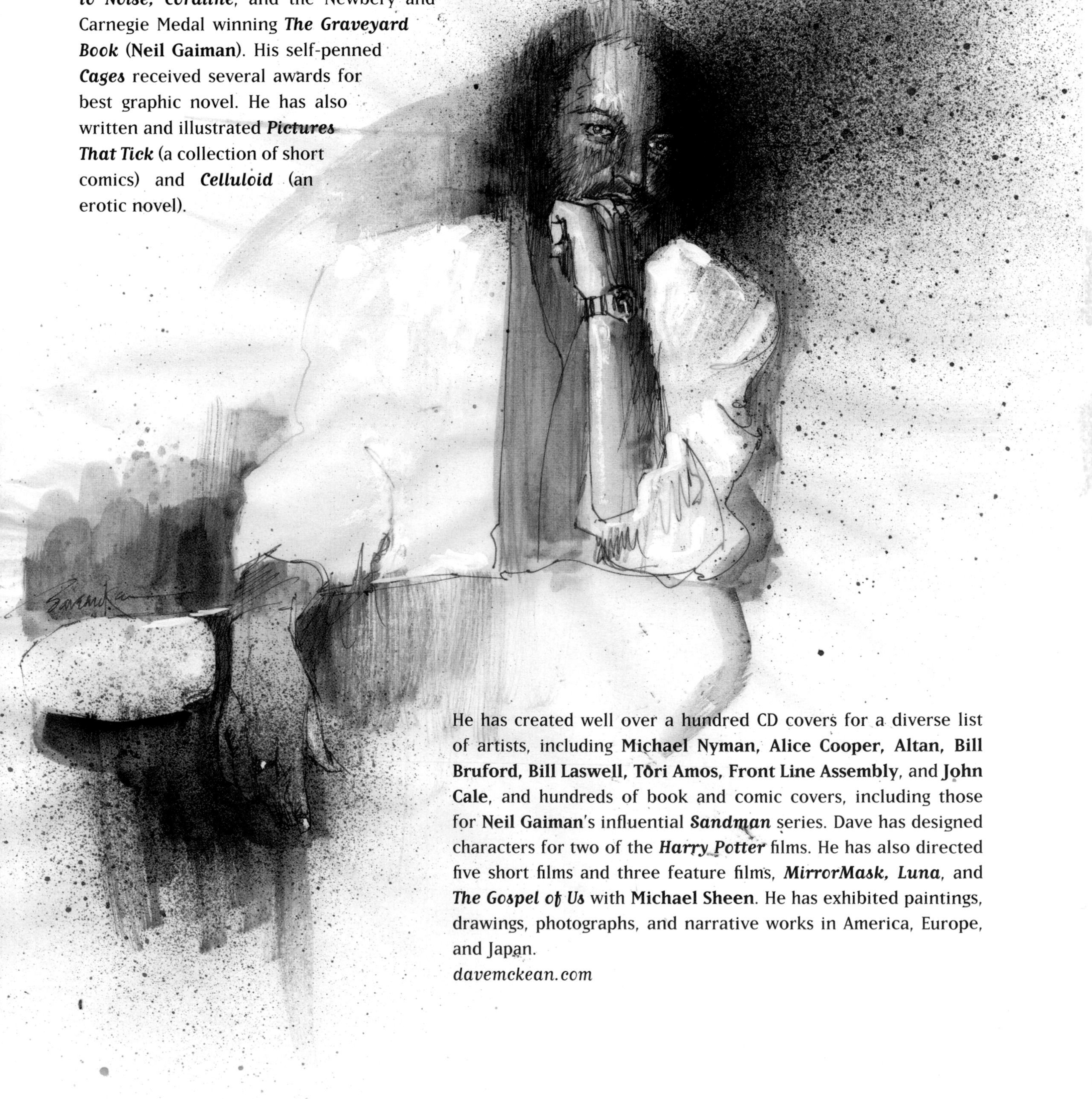

He has created well over a hundred CD covers for a diverse list of artists, including **Michael Nyman, Alice Cooper, Altan, Bill Bruford, Bill Laswell, Tori Amos, Front Line Assembly**, and **John Cale**, and hundreds of book and comic covers, including those for **Neil Gaiman**'s influential ***Sandman*** series. Dave has designed characters for two of the ***Harry Potter*** films. He has also directed five short films and three feature films, ***MirrorMask, Luna***, and ***The Gospel of Us*** with **Michael Sheen**. He has exhibited paintings, drawings, photographs, and narrative works in America, Europe, and Japan.

davemckean.com

MORE TITLES FROM
NEIL GAIMAN AND DAVE MCKEAN . . .

Signal to Noise
Neil Gaiman, Dave McKean
ISBN 978-1-59307-752-5
$24.99

Pictures That Tick
Dave McKean
ISBN 978-1-59582-328-1
$24.99

Pictures That Tick Volume 2
Dave McKean
ISBN 978-1-61655-308-1
$29.99

Cages
Dave McKean
ISBN 978-1-59582-316-8
$29.99

Harlequin Valentine
Neil Gaiman, John Bolton
ISBN 978-1-56971-620-5
$12.95

Last Temptation
Neil Gaiman, Michael Zulli
ISBN 978-1-59307-414-2
$14.95

The Facts in the Case of the Departure of Miss Finch
Neil Gaiman, Michael Zulli
ISBN 978-1-59307-667-2
$13.95

To find a comics shop in your area, call 1-888-266-4226
For more information or to order direct:
On the web: DarkHorse.com
E-mail: mailorder@darkhorse.com
Phone: 1-800-862-0052 Mon–Fri 9 am to 5 pm Pacific Time

DarkHorse.com

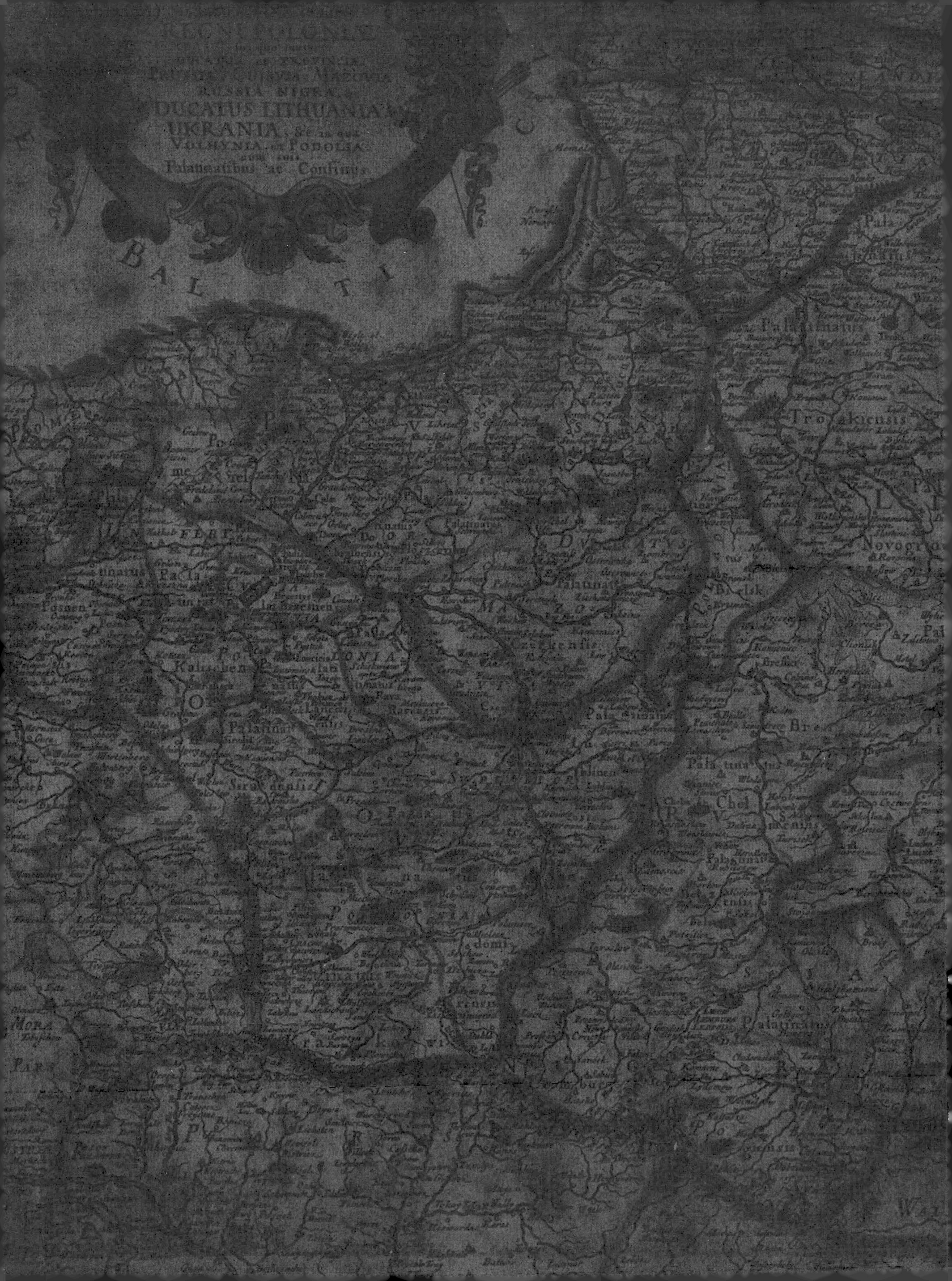
DUCATUS LITHUANIAE
UKRANIA
VOLHYNIA
PODOLIA
Palatinatibus ac Confiniis
BALTI
Palatinatus
Trokiensis
DUCATUS
MAZO
Palatinatus